ALTER
YOUR LIFE

ALTER YOUR LIFE

EMMET FOX

HarperSanFrancisco
A Division of HarperCollins*Publishers*

FIRST HARPERCOLLINS PAPERBACK EDITION PUBLISHED IN 1994

Library of Congress Cataloging-in-Publication Data

Fox, Emmet.
    Alter your life / Emmet Fox. — 1st HarperCollins pbk. ed.
    p. cm.
Originally published: New York: Harper & Row, 1931.
ISBN 0–06–250897–0 (pbk. : alk. paper)
1. New Thought   I. Title
BF639.F6718 1994   93–23918
248.4'8998—dc20   CIP

93 94 95 96 97 ❖ CWI 9 8 7 6 5 4 3 2 1
This edition is printed on acid-free paper that meets the American National Standards Institute Z39.48 Standard.

Contents

OTHER WRITINGS BY EMMET FOX

The Sermon on the Mount
Le Sermon sur la Montagne
El Sermon del Monte
Power Through Constructive Thinking
Find and Use Your Inner Power
Make Your Life Worth While

Alter Your Life

T HERE is no need to be unhappy. There is no
need to be sad. There is no need to be disappointed, or oppressed, or aggrieved. There is
no need for illness or failure or discouragement. There
is no *necessity* for anything but success, good health, prosperity, and an abounding interest and joy in life.

That the lives of many people are full of dreary things
is unfortunately only too true; but there is no *necessity* for
them to be there. They are there only because their victims suppose them to be inevitable, not because they are
so. As long as you accept a negative condition at its own
valuation, so long will you remain in bondage to it; but
you have only to assert your birthright as a free man or
woman and you will be free.

Success and happiness are the natural condition of
mankind. It is actually easier for us to demonstrate these
things than the reverse. Bad habits of thinking and acting
may obscure this fact for a time, just as a wrong way of
walking or sitting, or holding a pen or a musical instrument may seem to be easier than the proper way, because

1

we have accustomed ourselves to it; but the proper way is the easier nevertheless.

Unhappiness, frustration, poverty, loneliness are really bad habits that their victims have become accustomed to bear with more or less fortitude, believing that there is no way out, whereas there is a way; and that way is simply to acquire good habits of mind instead of bad ones— habits of working with the Law instead of against it.

You should never "put up" with anything. You should never be willing to accept less than Health, Harmony, and Happiness. These things are your Divine Right as the sons and daughters of God, and it is only a bad habit, unconscious, as a rule, that causes you to be satisfied with less. In the depths of his being man always feels intuitively that there is a way out of his difficulties if only he can find it, and his natural instincts all point in the same direction. The infant, as yet uncontaminated by the defeatist suggestions of his elders, simply refuses to tolerate inharmony on any terms, and therefore he demonstrates over it. When he is hungry he tells the world with a confident insistence that commands attention, while many a sophisticated adult goes without. Does he find a pin sticking in some part of his anatomy? Not for him a sigh of resignation to the supposed "will of God" (it is really blasphemy to say that evil or suffering could ever be the will of God, All Good), or a whine about never having any luck, or a sigh that what cannot be cured must be endured. No, the defeatist view of life has not yet touched him; his instincts tell him that life and harmony are inseparable. And sure enough, that pin is located and removed even if everything else has to come to a stop until it is done.

But "shades of the prison-house begin to close about the growing boy," and by the time he is old enough to think rationally the Race habit will have trained him to use his reason largely in the inverted way.

Refuse to tolerate anything less than harmony. You can have prosperity no matter what your present circumstances may be. You can have health and physical fitness. You can have a happy and joyous life. You can have a good home of your own. You can have congenial friends and comrades. You can have a full, free, joyous life, independent and untrammeled. You can become your own master or your own mistress. But to do this you must definitely seize the rudder of your own destiny and steer boldly and firmly for the port that you intend to make.

What are *you* doing about your future? Are you content to let things just drift along as they are, hoping, like Mr. Micawber, for something to "turn up"? If you are, be assured that there is no escape in that way. Nothing ever will turn up unless you exercise your Free Will and go out and turn it up for yourself by becoming acquainted with the Laws of Life, and applying them to your own individual conditions. That is the only way. Otherwise the years will pass all too swiftly, leaving you just where you are now, if not worse off, for there is no limit to the result of thought either for good or evil.

Man has dominion over all things when he knows the Law of Being, and obeys it. The Law gives you power to bring any condition into your life that is not harmful. The Law gives you power to overcome your own weaknesses and faults of character, no matter how often you may have failed in the past or how tenacious they may have seemed to be. The Law gives you power to attain prosperity and position without infringing the rights and opportunities of anyone else in the world. The Law gives you Freedom; freedom of soul, and body, and environment.

The Law gives you Independence so that you can build your own life in your own way, in accordance with your own ideas and ideals; and plan out your future along the lines that you yourself desire. <u>If you do not know what you really want to make you happy, then the Law will tell you what you want,</u> and get it for you too. <u>And the Law rightly understood and applied will save you from the danger of what is called "outlining" with all its risks and limitations</u>.

The Law will endow you with the gift of what is called Originality; Originality is the doing of things in a new way which is a better way, and different from anyone else's way; and Originality, as distinct from its counterfeits which are eccentricity and mere posing, means success in your work.

The Law will give you authority over the past as well as the future. The Law will make you the master of Karma instead of its slave.

Oh, how I love Thy Law.

You need not be shabby and restricted. You need not go on living or working with people you dislike. You need not be ailing or tired or overworked, <u>if you will study the Law and apply it</u>.

Do not "put off" your study of the Law any longer. Procrastination, we are told, is the thief of time; and another proverb says still more emphatically that Hell itself is paved, not with evil intentions, but with good ones.

It is of the postponer that the Law says, *Thou shalt hear the Never Never whispered by the phantom years,* but the path of the Wise (the righteous or Right Thinker) shineth more and more unto the Perfect Day.

<u>Take stock of your life this very day.</u> Sit down quietly by yourself with a pencil and paper, and write down the

three things that you most wish for in life. Be quite frank about this. Write down the things you *really* wish for, not things that you think you *ought* to wish for. Be specific, not vague. Then write down underneath three things or conditions that you wish to *remove* from your life. Again, be definite and specific, and not vague.

If you do this candidly, you now have an extremely valuable analysis of your own mentality. In course of time this will tell you a great many things about yourself which you do not at present suspect, things far beyond the range of the actual six points themselves and as your knowledge of spiritual Truth increases, you will be able to handle the new knowledge about yourself in a surprising way.

Now having got your six points in front of you, work on each one separately for a few minutes with all the spiritual and metaphysical knowledge that you possess. Remember, it is not really very important how much of this knowledge you have so long as you make use of all that you do have. It is a spiritual law that to use 90 percent of a small amount of knowledge is more practically effective than to use only say 50 percent of a large amount. Repeat this treatment every day for a month, without missing a single day, and by the end of that time it will be very unusual if a really striking change for the better has not manifested itself in your conditions.

For those unfamiliar with spiritual treatment, a simple but quite effective method of working is this: Claim gently but definitely that the Great Creative Life Force of the Universe is bringing each of the first three things into your life in Its own way, in Its own time, and in Its own form. Then claim that the same Great Power is dissolving each of the latter three, also in Its own way. Do not try to dictate the exact form in which the new conditions shall come about. Do not be tense or vehement. Do not let anyone else know that you are doing this. Do not look impatiently every day for results, but make your treatment, and forget it until next day. *And in quietness and confidence shall be your strength.*

The Four
Horsemen of the Apocalypse

T HE Four Horsemen of the Apocalypse are among the most important of the great Bible symbols because they give the key to the nature of man as we know him. When you understand these symbols thoroughly you will understand your own make-up, and you will be able to begin the work of getting dominion over yourself and over your surroundings.

There is another reason why it is important to understand the Four Horsemen. They form a typical example of the way in which the Bible makes use of the general principle of symbolism. When you have grasped their full significance, by realizing how the Bible talks about horses, for instance, in order to teach psychological and spiritual truth, you will have mastered the general scheme of Bible allegory. The Bible is not written in the style of a modern book. It has a method all its own of conveying knowledge through picturesque symbols, the reason being that this is the only possible way in which knowledge could be given to people in all ages in different parts of the world and of different degrees of spiritual development. A direct statement in the modern manner would appeal to a particular kind of audience, but a symbol appeals to any audience, each individual getting just what he is ready for.

The Bible is not full of predictions. The Bibles does not undertake to say just what is going to happen in the future, because if this could be done it could only mean that we have no free will. If the future is all arranged now—like a movie film packed in its box—what would be the use of praying or studying metaphysics? Why did Jesus pray for so many hours, even all night long, if he could not change anything? But, of course, you can change the future and the present by prayer, and, indeed, it is your attitude toward prayer that makes or mars you—makes you sick or well, happy or sad, stupid or wise.

The Four Horsemen of the Apocalypse[1] stand for the four parts or elements of our human nature as we find it today. As we know ourselves in our present embodiment we seem to be made up of four parts. There is, first of all, the physical body—the thing that you see when you look into the glass. Then there is your feeling nature or emotions. This is an extremely important part of you, and although you cannot "see" your feelings, you are tremendously conscious of them. Third, there is your intellect. You cannot see this either, but you are quite aware of its existence, because it contains every bit of knowledge, important or unimportant, that you possess.

Finally, there is your spiritual nature, or your real eternal self; the true you, the I AM, the Indwelling Christ, the Divine Spark, or what you please to call it. This is your

---

1. Revelation 6.

real identity, which is eternal. Almost everyone believes in
its existence, but for the most part people are very little
conscious of it as an actuality.

Students of metaphysics are aware that ultimately the
time will come when the first three will be merged in the
fourth, and then we shall all *know* instead of only *believing* that the spiritual nature is all. Meanwhile, however, this
is not the case, and so we find ourselves living with these
four elements of our nature—and the Bible calls them the
Four Horses.

The first horse we shall consider is the Pale Horse and
"pale" means the color of terror. Perhaps you have seen
terror depicted on a human countenance—I do not mean
just nervousness or moderate fear, but terror. It is not a
pleasant sight. The skin turns a kind of ashen gray, and
that is the color of the Pale Horse.

*And his name that sat on him was Death, and Hell followed
after him.*[2]

Well, the Pale Horse means the physical body, and here
we are told that he who rides on him is Death, and that
Hell follows hard after. If you are that kind of horseman,
if you live but for the body, there is nothing but hell
awaiting you on this plane or anywhere else. People who
live for the body are to be pitied. The body is the most
cruel taskmaster of all, when it is allowed to be the ruler.
The person who lives for eating and drinking and sensuality brings nothing but evil and destruction into his
life right here on this plane. Remember that the person
who lives for the body cannot be regenerating and therefore he is getting older every year. That means that the
body is steadily failing, and he has no other resources.
To him old age brings decrepitude and emptiness, and

2. Revelation 6:8.

probably pain and discomfort too. He has ridden the Pale Horse, and hell must follow that horseman.

But the Pale Horse does not mean only the physical body. It means all other physical things too—what the Bible sometimes calls the "world"—money, position, material honors.

If you put money before everything else, you are riding the Pale Horse even though you are not a glutton or a sensualist. Money is your God, and you will probably get it, but you will be sorry—because hell follows after. Why worship money? After you have bought a little food, a little clothing, paid your rent, and got a few other things, what can money give you? There are millionaires walking down Fifth Avenue who find that there is not a single thing they really need that their money can buy for them. They cannot walk into any store with a blank check and purchase peace of mind, or a healthy body, or friendship, or loyalty, or, above all, a contact with God.

Other people again do not care for money, but they do crave worldly honor and distinction. They want to be important or, it is more accurate to say, they want to be considered important. They want to be the Head of something. They want to be looked up to. They are not thinking of how much good they can do in the world, but of how much honor they can receive. They too are riding the Pale Horse, and hell follows after. If you could read the hearts of those that sit in the seats of the mighty you would be surprised how often you would discover disappointment and chagrin—for the Pale Horse always runs true to form.

If a person accepts an important office because he honestly wants to serve others and to glorify God, he is not on the Pale Horse, and in his case, if things go wrong or he is misunderstood or abused, he does not care. It does not grieve him, because he was trying to do God's work and that is true success.

He who lives to eat and drink, the sensualist and the drug addict; he who lives for money or worldly honors; is the rider on the Pale Horse.

Next I am going to take the Red Horse.[3]

And there went out another horse that was red; and power was given to him that sat thereon to take peace from the earth, and that they should kill one another: and there was given unto him a great sword.

What is the Red Horse? The Red Horse is your emotional nature, your feelings. Your human mind, as you know it, consists of two parts, intellect and feeling, and there is nothing else. Every thought that you can think has two parts, a knowledge content and a feeling content; and so you always get these two things, knowledge and feeling. Knowledge belongs to the intellect, and feeling, of course, to the emotional nature. In some thoughts the knowledge content is much greater than the feeling content, and in other thoughts it is the feeling content that is greater.

In mathematics, to take an extreme case, the feeling content is almost absent. No one gets very emotional over the knowledge that any two sides of a triangle are together greater than the third side, or that when two straight lines intersect the vertically opposite angles are equal. A small emotional content does exist because definite and certain knowledge always gives a little satisfaction to the mind, and there is also a certain beauty in these mathematical truths; but it is still true that for most people the amount of feeling would be quite small.

---

3. Revelation 6:4.

On the other end of the scale are thoughts connected with religion and politics. We all know how full of feeling (not to say prejudice) these subjects are. People feel so strongly about them that they are generally tabooed at social gatherings—and yet the amount of real knowledge that most people have concerning them is surprisingly small. For instance, few people have really studied the doctrines of the particular church to which they belong. Yet they feel very strongly about them and are apt to resent the slightest criticism concerning them. Few people have carefully considered the political principle underlying their own political party, nor have they taken the trouble to familiarize themselves with very much data on the subject, in spite of which they will be heatedly partisan. On these and other questions people have a mass of feeling almost unenlightened by the intellect. The intellectual content of such thoughts is very small.

It is very dangerous to allow your emotions to have control—to allow the Red Horse to run away with you, for he will undermine your health and wreck your life in every phase. The Red Horse is just as dangerous as the Pale Horse, but of course he is not so base, and for this reason he wrecks many more lives. An adult person is a person who has control of his feelings. A person who cannot control his feelings is still a child, even though he be a hundred years old. If you cannot control your emotion, your emotion will control you and wreck you.

This does not mean that emotion or feeling is a bad thing in itself. It means that *uncontrolled* emotion is a bad thing. As a matter of fact, it is almost as bad to have too little emotion as too much. People who are emotionally weak never amount to anything. They are those very nice people who are never considered or even noticed. No one knows or cares whether they are in the room or not.

They drift into life seemingly by accident; they drift into a business where they never amount to anything; they drift into marriage; and finally they drift into the grave—all seemingly more or less by inadvertence.

A strong emotional nature is like a great powerful automobile. If you control it, it is a fine thing. It will take you wherever you want to go, through the roughest country, or to the top of a mountain, because it is full of power. But if you do not control it, if you do not understand how to steer it, or if you are stupid and step on the gas when you ought to step on the brake, the car destroys itself and you with it, just because it is so powerful.

If you get an old feeble car which can hardly chug along it won't get you anywhere, but it won't do you any harm either. Even if you run it up against a wall it only coughs and stops.

A strong emotional nature is a splendid endowment if you are the master, but if it is mastering you, you are riding the Red Horse; and if you are riding the Red Horse you had better get off as soon as possible. There is no salvation for that horseman.

How do you know if you are riding the Red Horse? Well, if you get excited over nothing at all, if you get angry and indignant about trifles, particularly when it happens to be none of your business; if you get worked up over things you read in the newspaper; if you are trying to run other people's lives and getting excited about that, then you are riding the Red Horse—and you had better get off.

The time when you learn to control your feelings is the time you will begin to make something of your life.

Next I come to the Black Horse and here it says:

And I beheld, and lo a black horse; and he that sat on him had a pair of balances in his hand. And I heard a voice in the midst

of the four beasts say, A measure of wheat for a penny, and three
measures of barley for a penny.[4]

A pair of scales, that is, a balance such as a grocer or a
druggist uses, is here a symbol of famine or lack. It means
that there is not enough to go round and therefore that
things have to be rationed. The Black Horse stands for the
intellect, and if you ride the Black Horse you will get
famine or starvation of the soul. Very few people ride
the Black Horse as compared with the number of those
who ride the Red one, but some do, and the civilized
world as a whole has been riding it for several centuries.

To ride the Black Horse does not mean having a good
intellect. That is not a bad thing at all. In fact, a great
many people, particularly in the religious world, would
be much better off with a little more intellect than they
have. Riding the Black Horse is letting your intellect dominate you to the exclusion of the emotional, and especially of the spiritual, nature. It is a good thing to have the
intellect well trained and polished by use, but it is a misfortune to let it be the master. There are people who say
that the universe can be understood intellectually—that
everything about God can be put into plain English and
explained precisely in words. This is absurd because it is
really an attempt to define the Infinite, and, as Spinoza
says, to define God is to deny Him. Other people dog-
matize and say that nothing exists but matter and that
mind is a secretion of matter, and that therefore mind
cannot dominate matter, and man cannot survive death
because he cannot take his body with him. These people say that the brain thinks, and that when the brain
rots in the grave, the thinker cannot be alive. There are
other people who would resent being called materialists,

---

4. Revelation 6:5–6.

yet they say that they cannot believe in prayer because
the laws of nature are deterministic and therefore prayer
could not possibly change anything.

All these people are riding the Black Horse and they
suffer famine because such mistaken beliefs starve them
of all spiritual understanding and growth.

Intellect is an excellent thing, and indeed we could
not live on this plane without it; but intellect can only
deal with three-dimensional things. Beyond that it breaks
down. We must have the intellect for buying and selling,
for putting up buildings and making roads, for doing
our daily work, in short; but as we approach God, we
leave the territory of the intellect and go beyond it into
the region of the spiritual, where the values are perfection and dimension is infinity. The truth about God must
go beyond the intellect and it calls for the spiritual nature
to understand it. The instrument of the intellect is reason, and while it is true that anything that contradicts
reason cannot be true, the truths of religion must go beyond reason though without, of course, contradicting it.

The intellect cannot give you the truth about God,
and to suppose that it can is like trying to use a ther-
mometer to weigh a package or to try to use a pair of
scales to measure the temperature of the room. When
you do that you are confusing your instruments.

If you try to live without knowledge of God, without
prayer or spiritual contact, you are certain sooner or
later to reach a condition of depression and disappointment, for that is the fate of the Horseman on the
Black Horse.

In the nineteenth century many men of science did
not believe in anything that could not be isolated in a
test tube or examined under the microscope. These ma-
terialistic scientists rode the Black Horse; but today some

of the most eminent natural scientists are beginning to recognize the existence of spiritual things.

Western civilization has been definitely riding the Black Horse since the close of the Middle Ages. The Renaissance rediscovered the intellect and that was a splendid achievement, but Western civilization did not keep the intellect in its place. It was allowed to become the master. Ever since then our form of education has been predominantly intellectual, to the neglect of other things. Especially has this been the case since the Modern Age began with the invention of a commercially practicable steam engine in the middle of the eighteenth century.

The recent World War, which was in reality but a continuation of the previous World War, was directly due to this policy. Humanity has developed scientific, intellectual knowledge far beyond the point to which it has developed the moral and spiritual understanding of the race. This development has given man the power to make high explosives, for example, and to build submarines and aircraft, but because his spiritual development has lagged so far behind his intellectual achievements, he uses these things for destruction and tyranny. Had the understanding of true religion kept pace with scientific discovery, such knowledge would be used for the enlightenment and happiness of mankind instead of for its destruction. All this is riding the Black Horse.

The Horseman on the Black Horse is like the pilot who spends the whole day taxiing around the ground— never soaring up. Now a plane is not built to run on the ground. Even the cheapest and oldest automobile will go better on the ground than the best airplane. The plane is built not for the ground, but for flying through the sky, and until it does leave the ground it is not in its element.

Finally, I come to the fourth horse, and here we have the solution of all our problems.

And I saw, and behold a white horse: and he that sat on him had a bow; and a crown was given unto him: and he went forth conquering, and to conquer.[5]

The White Horse is the Spiritual Nature, and the man or woman who rides the White Horse gets freedom, and joy, and ultimate happiness and harmony; because the White Horse is the realization of the Presence of God. When you put God first in your life, when you refuse to limit God, when you will no longer say that God cannot do something, when you trust God with your whole heart, *you are riding the White Horse,* and it is only a question of time until you shall be free—when the day will break and the shadows flee away. The White Horse will carry you to health and freedom and self-expression; to a knowledge of God, and finally to the Realization of Him. On the White Horse you will go forth conquering and to conquer.

We are told two very interesting things about the Horseman on the White Horse: the Bible says that he that sat on him had a bow. The bow and arrow is an ancient symbol of the spoken Word. The spoken Word brings things to pass. When you speak the Word you shoot an arrow. It goes where you aim it and it cannot be recalled, nor can it return void. Note that the Word does not have to be spoken audibly. Silent prayer is usually more powerful than audible prayer, but if you find it hard to concentrate because you are worried or afraid, you will find it easier to pray audibly. The Horseman on the White Horse speaks the Word.

---

5. Revelation 6:2.

The rider on the White Horse wears a crown, and the crown has always been the symbol of victory. Whoever wins in a struggle gets the crown. The Greeks used to give a crown of palms to the winner of a race, and all through history kings have been crowned. The crown is a symbol of victory, and the rider on the White Horse is always the victor.

This, then, is the story of the Four Horsemen of the Apocalypse. If you want peace of mind, if you want healing, happiness, prosperity, and freedom; above all, if you want an understanding of God, there is only one way—you must ride the White Horse.

If you are interested only in material things, or if you are letting your emotions run away with you, or if you are trying to judge eternal values by finite intellectual standards, you are riding one of the other horses and only trouble can come to you.

The fatal defect in the Roman Empire was that it rode the Pale Horse, and we know what happened to it. Our own civilization for about four hundred years has ridden the Black Horse, and we see what has come of that. Now, however, I believe that humanity is ready, or very nearly ready, to climb upon the White Horse, and we must all help it to do so in every way that we can by prayer and by personal example. The Horseman on the White Horse goes forth conquering and to conquer.

This, then, is the way in which human nature, as we know it, is made up. We seem to have four elements, but as a student of metaphysics you know that only one of these is real and eternal. This, of course, is your spiritual nature. Some day you will realize this and then the other elements will fade away into nothing, leaving you spiritual, complete, and perfect. That event, however, will not come yet; and in the meantime you have

to understand your fourfold nature in order that you
may control it.

This fourfold constitution of man is also taught in the
Bible in other ways. For instance, the four beasts of Revelation[6] are really the four horses treated in another and
most interesting way. We find here a lion, a calf (or ox or
bull), a third beast with the face of a man, and a flying
eagle.

Here, the second beast "like a calf" represents the body
and the physical plane in general and takes the place of
the Pale Horse. The third beast "had a face as a man,"
and represents intellect or the Black Horse. It has been
traditional to have the face, and especially the forehead,
stand for intellect, just as the heart stands for the feelings. The fourth beast "was like a flying eagle" and he
represents the emotional nature, or the Red Horse. The
first beast was "like a lion" and represents the spiritual
nature, or the White Horse.

These different references in the Bible are not mere
repetitions or restatements, for each one treats the subject from a slightly different angle and thereby gives us further knowledge. We see here, for instance, that the
emotional nature is expressed by an eagle. This represents Scorpio in the Zodiac, and Scorpio may be expressed either by a reptile (sometimes a scorpion and
sometimes a snake) or an eagle. The lesson here again is
that the emotional nature has to be redeemed by trans-
muting the lower into the higher so that the once crawl-
ing reptile becomes a soaring eagle. Only then will you
have dominion over it. You will see that this is a much
higher and fuller statement of the subject than the mere

6. Revelation 4:6–9; Ezekiel 1·10 10·14

comparison to a Red Horse, although that was striking and useful to begin with.

It is interesting to note here that the symbol of an eagle with the snake in its mouth (conquering the snake) is still used in Mexico. An old Aztec legend said that when the people entered the new land (modern Mexico) they were to march on until they found an eagle devouring a snake. At that point they were to build their city—and thus was chosen the site of the Mexico City of today.

The Aztecs undoubtedly derived this legend from their Atlantean ancestors, and the real meaning would be that The City, the true consciousness, can only be built when the emotional nature has been transmuted.

The ox (sometimes a calf or a bull) is obvious as the symbol of materiality. It is traditionally dull, heavy, and earthy, and was used in the Old World for the useful but commonplace work of pulling the plow. The ox does not soar like the eagle, think like the man's head, or lead the kingly life of a lion.

The lion, the king of beasts, well represents the spiritual nature, and corresponds to the White Horse.

These four beasts are at the throne of God where there is "a sea of glass like unto crystal." We are always at the throne of God, although we know it not, for He is everywhere, and our separation from Him, tragic as it seems, is only a separation in belief. The sea of glass means a sea as smooth as a sheet of glass, and this is the consciousness which has gotten away from *fear*—which has subdued the ox, changed the reptile into an eagle, redeemed the intellect, and enthroned the lion.

"The four beasts had each of them six wings." In the Bible the number six stands for labor or work and this means that we have to work out our salvation by constant vigilance in seeking God and overcoming self. We must

not wait in idleness for God to come and do it for us; because there is no attainment without work. If you want
anything you must work for it. We find this meaning given
to the number six in many parts of the Bible. The number six comes before the number seven, and the number seven stands, in the Bible, for individual perfection
in the life of a man, and for a particular demonstration
where that demonstration is complete. We find six days
of creation leading to the seventh day of rest in attainment; six steps to the throne of Solomon, who stands for
wisdom or the understanding of God; six pots of water at
the marriage of Cana; and, of course, six working days
of the week leading to the Sabbath.[7]

The wings enabled the beasts to soar from the ground,
and again there are six of them because liberation has
to be earned. We must seek God day and night. To say
Holy, Holy, Holy, is, in our modern language, to see the
Presence of God everywhere, instead of accepting the
appearance of evil.

"Which was, and is, and is to come," means that we
have to realize that we are in eternity now, because the belief in the reality of time is one of the principal errors
that hold us in bondage.

The four beasts are "full of eyes before and behind"
and that is only another way of telling us that we must
exercise unceasing vigilance in the Practice of the Presence of God.

Outside of the Bible we find many references to the
four-fold constitution of man. In the ancient world they
invariably referred to the four parts as "Elements," and
called them earth, air, water, and fire. Earth meant the
physical body; air meant the intellect; water meant the

7. And see Isaiah 6.

feeling nature; and fire meant the spiritual or divine part of us. It was thought best for many reasons not to give all this knowledge openly to the general public, but to hide it behind the veil of such symbols and to give the key only to those who were ready for it.

The Zodiac[8] which may be called the Cosmic Clock, is divided up in this way. Of the twelve Signs, three are allotted to each element, and they thus form a graph or picture diagram of man.

The idea of these four elements is also expressed in the traditional symbols for the four Gospels. Matthew is represented by an ox or calf. The lion of St. Mark is familiar to all. John has an eagle, and for Luke a man's face is the accepted symbol. This tradition goes back to the earliest times and these creatures appear, each attached to his own Gospel, in many of the illuminated manuscripts of the Middle Ages and in the stained glass windows of the earliest cathedrals in Europe.

Here we get a still higher development of the lesson of the four elements because, just as the Gospels are the highest expression of the Christian message, so these symbols give us the final statement concerning the method of man's overcoming.

Matthew takes people as he finds them on the material plane, assumes their customs and traditions, and, meeting them on their own level, gives them the Gospel in the way that he thinks they can receive it. The physical body and the material world of which it is a part, are with us for the time being, and we have to tolerate them and handle them as well as we can. You will see how well this idea is expressed by the element Earth (ox).

_____

8. See the chapter, "The Zodiac and the Bible."

The Gospel of Mark is the most intellectual of the four. It is simple, direct, and businesslike as a military dispatch or an engineer's report; yet its symbol is the lion which as we have seen stands for the spiritual element. Why is this? The object is to teach us that the intellect has ultimately to be absorbed by the spiritual nature, not that the intellect will really be destroyed but that it will lose its limitations and become Illumined Intelligence. The reader should here note the immense difference between the words intelligence and intellect. Intellect is only a small and narrow segment of intelligence. There are many forms of intelligence that are not intellectual although the modern world forgot this for a time.

The Gospel of Luke represents the emotional nature. It is often called the "human" Gospel because of its kindly understanding of and toleration for human nature, and because of its liberal attitude toward the Gentiles and toward women, an attitude not characteristic of most ancient writers. It is symbolized, however, by the face of a man which we know is the symbol for intellect, and the profound idea behind this fact is this, namely, that the student on the path has first to learn to make his emotional nature subject to his intellect. He has to make that which he knows control that which he feels. After that will come the spiritualization of both elements.

The Gospel of John stands for the spiritual nature and is the highest of the Gospels as well as the most profound. It is symbolized, not by the lion as one might expect, but by the eagle. As we have seen, the eagle is the emotional nature redeemed and purified, and when this transmutation has taken place, it too is absorbed in the spiritual nature.

It is necessary to note that in some instances the symbols for Matthew and Luke have been mistakenly interchanged.

This was done at some time by people who did not understand the meaning behind them and was originally probably a copyist's error. The slightest reflection will show that the ox does not fit Luke nor does the human face, the symbol of all mankind, belong to the restricted outlook of Matthew.

To sum up then, we have to take ourselves as we find ourselves here and now, without unnecessary regret or self-condemnation. We have to become master of the body, and of the physical plane in general. We have to make the emotional nature subservient to the intellect in order that both emotions and intellect may be transformed into the spiritual. To human perception these processes go on at the same time, and when they are complete, the earth plane disappears from consciousness and Spirit is all. This is what is called translation, dematerialization, or the ascension demonstration. You will see that the story is told in a subtle but very clear way by the Gospel symbols.

The four elements are also referred to in Daniel's story of the three men thrown into the fiery furnace.[9] That chapter is a parable of human nature redeemed. The characters took their ordeal or initiation successfully, and the result was the appearance of a fourth man "like unto the Son of God." That was the emergence of the spiritual nature.

A remarkable treatment of the four elements is given in the Book of Numbers, Chapter 2. It is concerned with the marshalling of the Twelve Tribes of Israel in the great camp around the Tabernacle in the wilderness. The Tabernacle in the wilderness represents the human body and mind at the stage when we are still in the wilderness,

---

9. Daniel 3:25.

which means that we have gotten out of Egypt (no longer believe that outer things really have power over us) but have not yet been able to prove it by demonstrating all-round harmony in practice, which is, of course, the present condition of most students of metaphysics.

The Twelve Tribes are drawn up in camp to correspond with the signs of the Zodiac; for each of the tribes was symbolized by one of the Signs, and carried it as a banner or totem at the head of the ranks when they marched.

It may seem strange to the reader that the Signs of the Zodiac should be brought into this at all, but, of course, we have to take the Bible as we find it. These things are in the Bible, and it is our business to interpret the Bible rather than to think it should have been written in some other way.

Judah represents the spiritual element (Leo—Fire) and is placed "on the east side toward the rising of the sun."[10] The east traditionally stands for God. The historical Christian churches and most pagan temples are *oriented*. The altar is in the east and the usual custom is to bury the dead with their feet toward the east so that the body shall face that way. Thus, it is entirely natural that the Bible should put Judah in the east.

Reuben[11] represents the physical body or the Pale Horse (Taurus—Earth). He is placed in the south because that is where the sun shines. (The Bible, of course, was written for people living in the northern hemisphere.) The spiritual nature arising in the east must be focused on the physical body because that has to be redeemed. The body is not to be *denied* but redeemed. Religious

---

10. Numbers 2:3.
11. Numbers 2:10.

people generally have tended to curse the body, to regard it as something evil, and we know that when we curse a thing it strikes back and gives trouble. Humanity must not curse the body but must redeem it by learning to demonstrate perfect health and self-control. Many of the Christian mystics, for instance, neglected or crucified the body in the hope of thus reaching God; but they still failed to control it.

Reuben, like the Pale Horse, stands for all material and worldly conditions as well as the body itself. We are not to run away from the world—we are to learn to overcome it.[12] And so we allow the sunshine of Truth to shine upon material things.

There is another important lesson here. People too easily forget that material conditions are always changing, and that the only permanent thing is God and His self-expression. As a matter of fact, all worldly arrangements and the physical universe itself are as unstable as water and pass away like a dream. In the case of solid matter the change takes much longer to happen than it does in the case of liquids and so we are apt to think of solid objects as permanent, but nevertheless they are always changing and fading too. Buildings, bridges, cities, the shapes of mountains, and the courses of rivers, and the very continents themselves come and go in the course of time. We have to realize that all worldly conditions, good and bad, pass away sooner or later and that nothing permanent can be built here below. The curse of Reuben is "unstable as water: thou shalt not excel."

Coming around to the west side we find Ephraim[13] who represents the intellect. (Aquarius—Air). This is, of

---

12. John 17:15.
13. Numbers 2:18.

course, another phase of the Black Horse; and we know that the sun seems to disappear in the west leaving us in the darkness of night—and this is the condition that comes from riding the Black Horse. The intellect also has to be redeemed by the spiritual nature for the light "cometh out of the east and shineth unto the west."[14]

Finally we have Dan[15] on the north side, standing for the emotional nature or Red Horse (Scorpio-Water). It is not necessary to repeat what has already been said about the emotional nature and the need for gaining control of it. The north, in the occult tradition, stands for trouble, fear, and general disharmony. It is the cold and dark region as distinct from the sunny south. In the present state of humanity, man's life is ruled by his emotional nature, and he must recognize this. Without emotion there is no action. Wrong thoughts, unaccompanied by fear or ill feeling, do the possessor no harm—they are sterile. Right thoughts or treatments devoid of feeling do not demonstrate. They are void. The feeling nature is what matters, and yet the control of the emotions is the last thing that the average person tries to attain. He will seek far and wide for health for his body. He will make great sacrifices to get an education for his intellect. He will seek God, or at least recognize religion, perfunctorily. Yet he will fail to understand or refuse to face the fact that he must learn to control his feelings in order to attain any of these ends. He places that subject in the "cold north."

There is a remarkable point about the treatment of Dan in the Bible. He is omitted from the final triumphant gathering of the tribes in the book of Revelation.[16] At

---

14. Matthew 24:27.
15. Numbers 2:25.
16. Revelation 7:4–8.

that day—the day when man attains his realization of
God—the lower emotional nature will have been completely obliterated and the higher emotional nature
merged in the spiritual. So that Dan drops out altogether.
Joseph, on his death bed, said, "Dan shall judge his people . . . Dan shall be a *serpent* by the way, an adder in the
path, that biteth the horse's heels, so that his rider shall
fall backward."[17] It is the lower emotional nature that is
the downfall of the vast majority of people. It strikes at the
"heel" or vulnerable spot in character, the part where
the individual "touches the ground," and it is glorious
to know that ultimately Dan will disappear.

The fourfold nature of the human being was taught
in ancient Egypt by means of the Sphinx. The Egyptians
inherited the idea from a previous civilization. There
were many ancient civilizations in the world which are
not yet known to our archaeologists. Man has lived in organized societies for tens of thousands of years, although
all traces of most of these civilizations have disappeared.
The Sphinx was probably Atlantean originally, and the
true Sphinx consists of the body of an animal (Earth-
Taurus), with a human face (Air—Aquarius). It has the
wings of an eagle (Water-Scorpio), and on the forehead
it carries the sacred device, the Ankh, which represents
spirit, the eternal Life (Fire—Leo).

Centuries afterward the Greeks copied the Sphinx,
but, not understanding the hidden import of the symbolism, they sometimes changed it to suit their artistic
preferences, giving it a woman's bust, and making other
changes. The Oedipus legend refers to the City of Thebes
which is in Greece, and is not concerned with the original and authentic Sphinx, which is Egyptian.

---

17. Genesis 49:16–17.

For modern readers it is especially interesting to note that outside the great Temple of the Sun at Heliopolis where Moses was a priest[18] there stood four great obelisks teaching the same lesson of the four elements. The priests would see them every time they passed in and out, and the location of the obelisks there at the entry implied that this knowledge is the portal to the understanding of God. In the intervening centuries these columns have been widely scattered, and, after a number of removals, one of them is today in Central Park, New York City, one in London on the Thames embankment, one in Constantinople, while the fourth still remains on the very spot where it was originally fixed, although all trace of the temple itself has disappeared. It is impossible not to feel a thrill of interest when we look at "Cleopatra's needle" as it is incorrectly called, when we walk through Central Park and try to realize that Moses himself often looked at that very column.

And so we have the same story told over and over again in the Bible and outside of it. Divine Mind has inspired individuals with this truth in all ages including the present one because it is the basis of all spiritual growth. The most important lesson to learn is the lesson of your own nature, for to understand that fully is to have the power to control it. Pythagoras wrote over the door of his school MAN KNOW THYSELF, and the Bible shows us how to do this.

---

18. Acts 7:22.

The Bond and the Free

 OR it is written, that Abraham had two sons, the one by a bondmaid, the other by a freewoman.

"But he who was of the bondwoman was born after the flesh; but he of the freewoman was by promise.

"WHICH THINGS ARE AN ALLEGORY: for these are the two covenants; the one from the mount Sinai, which gendereth to bondage, which is Agar.

"For this Agar is mount Sinai in Arabia, and answereth to Jerusalem which now is, and is in bondage with her children.

"But Jerusalem which is above is free, which is the mother of us all."

PAUL, GALATIANS 4:22–26

The Book of Genesis

G ENESIS means origin or beginning, and this, the first book of the Bible, explains how things and conditions come into existence. The creative power of the universe is thought. Anything that exists must first be thought of by someone before it can exist, and so all creation is but the concrete expression of thought.

Genesis deals with this creative power of thought. The first section, consisting of Chapter 1 and three verses of Chapter 2, deals with generic thought. The second chapter with which we are primarily concerned in this essay gives the story of Adam and Eve and deals with specific thought, or how a given person (you, the reader, for instance) builds every condition that exists in his life.

The following sections, concerning Cain and Abel, the tower of Babel, the flood, the story of Abraham and his family, the story of Joseph and his brethren, all deal in different ways with the creative power of thought, showing how it is the genesis of all things that exist. The Book of Genesis is partly allegorical and partly historical, but, as is always the case in the Bible, the historical portions are allegories too.

The object of the Bible is to teach psychology and metaphysics, or Spiritual Truth, so that we may know how to live aright. For this purpose allegories and parables are used that everyone may receive the teaching at the point of development where he is; and if the Bible is to be of any use, these parables must be interpreted spiritually.

Unless you have the spiritual meaning behind the story, you do not possess the Bible at all, you have only the "letter which killeth" and you lack "the spirit which giveth life." Paul, in the citation quoted above, compares one who has the letter only to the bondwoman, and the one who has the spiritual interpretation to the freewoman.

The spiritual interpretation of the Bible sets us free by teaching us how to bring health and harmony into our lives by an increased understanding of God. The covenant of Sinai, necessary and good in its place, signifies the attempt to order things from the outside and is, of course, much better than anarchy; but he who is on the spiritual path must pass beyond this to the spiritual Jerusalem which is the ordering of things from the inside by the Practice of the Presence of God. This is the new Jerusalem that cometh straight down from God out of heaven.[1]

The study of the spiritual key to the Bible changes our consciousness for the better, and it is this raising of the consciousness that makes the higher revelation possible to us.

The Book of Genesis having explained the creative power of thought, the other books of the Bible then proceed to illustrate the way in which the laws of thought work in different circumstances, but Genesis is the foundation of it all.

---

1. Revelation 3:12; 21:2; 21:10.

The Seven Days of Creation

T HE first chapter of Genesis lays a ground-plan for the entire revelation given in the Holy Scriptures. This chapter, and the first three verses of Chapter 2, are really one section; and this section constitutes a summary of the laws that govern thought. It is therefore a scientific treatise on the psychological and spiritual nature of man, and it explains what we call demonstration, or answer to prayer. It is not intended to be a history of the formation of the solar system or the stellar universe.

As a piece of literature the story is sublime; magnificent in range, in profundity of thought, and in the unparalleled heights of spiritual understanding which it attains. It shows how humanity as a race, and each individual personally, comes to a knowledge of the all-power, all-presence, and all-goodness of God.

The treatise is divided into seven parts, or seven days of creation. This arrangement expresses the seven stages through which thought passes in emerging from error to Truth.

At first there is darkness, or ignorance of those great truths which are really one Truth. Then, gradually, the light dawns, dim at first, but broadening slowly into clearer and clearer realization.

What we call nature is the outpicturing of a part of God's spiritual creation. It is true that we too often misinterpret what we see, or see it in a distorted way, but, as the light increases more and more, such misconceptions pass steadily away until the real truth is understood. This process is constantly symbolized for us by the dawn of each new morning. First we have darkness, then the first peep of light, and then the dawn comes up faster and faster until we emerge into the full day.

We can see that this is also the history of the coming into the knowledge of spiritual Truth by the individual. He begins with the belief of limitation and separateness, and then, at some time, through some means, the Truth is brought to him; and from a small beginning he gradually evolves into complete understanding.

Again, this is found to be the history of each individual demonstration. When a difficulty is solved, or a lack is satisfactorily filled, by prayer or spiritual treatment, we call it a demonstration, because it demonstrates the law of universal harmony. Well, it will be seen that the same process is gone through here—first the sense of limitation, then the turning to God and the gradual realization of His presence, which realization increases until the trouble disappears.

In the beginning God created the heaven and the earth. (Genesis 1:1)

The Bible starts by telling us that God is the Creator and beginning of everything. The first four words in the Bible are *In the beginning God.* A great lesson is given here, because any enterprise which is based on this principle must be successful in all respects.

We all know that God is outside of what we call "time"— *whose dwelling place is eternity.*[1] Therefore, in absolute truth, the universe, including ourselves, is being created afresh all the time. *Behold I make all things new.*[2] Nevertheless, while we are on this earth we all do believe, at least subconsciously, in the reality and power of time; and so, in terms of human thinking, we believe in God as the *beginning* of things.

And the earth was without form, and void; and darkness was upon the face of the deep. And the spirit of God moved upon the face of the waters. (Genesis 1:2)

God is the Creator of all things, and, therefore, all things that really exist are His expression; and they must and do reflect his perfection. This is the Truth, but, as we are aware, man does not at first know it. He uses his imagination negatively, to build up all kinds of limitation ideas, to produce all kinds of fears which, though really groundless, have power to cause him any amount of suffering, as long as he does believe them to be true. Good has an independent substantial existence whether we know about it or not, but evil has only the existence that we give it by believing in it. As long as we do believe in it, it seems to be just as real as if it were true. We experience just as much unhappiness as if it were true, just as the child in a nightmare suffers as much for the time being as if the dream were real. *God has made man upright but he has sought out many inventions.*[3]

---

1. Isaiah 57:15.
2. Revelation 21:5.
3. Ecclesiastes 7:29.

Thus, man lives in ignorance and fear, but one day the Truth of Being begins to dawn upon him—the Spirit of God moves upon the face of the waters—and his real history begins.

We note here that the Spirit of God moves on the face of the waters. Water, in the Bible, stands for the human mind—the intellect and the feelings—but in practice it is always the feeling nature that is the more important. It is not until the feelings are touched that something happens.

The text says, on the *face* of the waters. The face stands for the power of recognition. We usually recognize people by their faces, and the coming of light is the recognition of Truth.

First Day

And God said, Let there be light: and there was light.

And God saw the light, that it was good: and God divided the light from the darkness. (Genesis 1:3–4)

The first thing that this dawn of understanding does for man is to show him that there is a distinction between Truth and error. He knows now, however vaguely at first, that all experience is not equally authentic. This is one of the two or three greatest steps in his whole history. After this, fear can never again have quite the same power over him. This experience is called elsewhere in the Bible, "the First Resurrection," because man arises from the grave (tomb) of an existence without the knowledge of God.

And God called the light Day, and the darkness He called Night. And the evening and the morning were the first day. (Genesis 1:5)

Now that man has grasped the fact that all experience is not equally authentic, he begins to understand, however imperfectly, that good is powerful and error is not. Then, by active right thinking, by using his intuition and his reason, he can separate the wheat from the chaff. The good which is the Truth concerning anything, is here called *day* and the error and the fear that we attach to it are called *night*.

Thus, the First Day represents the dawn of spiritual consciousness. In the Bible, evening stands for limitation, fear, trouble, or lack of some needed good, and morning stands for fulfillment. The world usually reverses this, thinking rather of evening as fulfillment, culminating as it does in the unconsciousness of sleep. In the Bible, the dusk of evening leading to the darkness of night, is an erroneous state that must be forsaken. Twilight is only half light, or less. Man must work through it into the glory of the dawn.

Second Day

And God said, Let there be a firmament in the midst of the waters, and let it divide the waters from the waters.

And God made the firmament, and divided the waters which were under the firmament from the waters which were above the firmament: and it was so.

And God called the firmament Heaven. And the evening and the morning were the second day. (Genesis 1:6–8)

The firmament means understanding. Through the enlightenment, however dim, of the First Day, man has attained a beginning in understanding. To be aware, however vaguely, that error is illusion and without power, is his passport to paradise. He knows enough now, to put error outside the pale, so to speak. He will no longer willingly give it place in his scheme of things. He does not think that he knows much of the Truth yet, but he believes that that knowledge can be attained and that it will be found to have nothing to do with evil.

To understand this symbol we need to know that the ancients thought of the sky as being literally a dome—probably made of some kind of metal—and placed over the earth like a great roof; and the Bible writer calls this the firmament, and uses it as a simile for understanding. Thus, the waters above the firmament, or outside the roof (outside the pale) mean error, fear, or false beliefs of any kind. Below, or inside the firmament (under the law) is the human being who has received the first gleams of enlightenment. He knows now, as we have seen, that appearances are not necessarily true, and that they need not be feared. He realizes how prone he is to create illusion for himself, and he understands that these illusions must be put outside the pale.

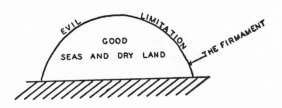

He knows that he himself is inside the pale, and that all Truth—and Truth only—is inside the pale. So his liberation has begun, his regeneration is under way, and, while he has much work in front of him to prove, by demonstration, the illumination that he has received, still he has received it. He knows that there is a way out, and he never again gives full credence to error. Henceforth, all his mental activity will be focused upon the study of Truth.

The rest of the chapter deals with his steady and increasing realization of Truth; and so the waters outside the firmament disappear from the narrative.

Third Day

And God said, Let the waters under the heaven be gathered together unto one place, and let the dry land appear: and it was so.

And God called the dry land Earth; and the gathering together of the waters called he Seas: and God saw that it was good. (Genesis 1:9–10)

Under the firmament, or within the Truth of Being, there are, of course, infinite ideas, and an infinite scope for man's true self-expression—which will naturally be the expression of God, since man's real destiny is to express God. "Under the firmament" it should be noted, is a purely figurative expression meaning anything that is true, and therefore real and under the law of harmony. It does not mean closed-in or circumscribed in any way. However big we might suppose the dome to be, it would still seem to enclose a limited area if we took it literally. Under the firmament is the infinite universe of God's perfect creation.

Obviously, even the most highly developed person has actually demonstrated only a very, very minute portion of available Truth. He knows *of* the existence of a number of other truths; that is to say, he knows intellectually of their existence as one may know *of* a country that he has not visited, or *of* a piece of beautiful music which he has not yet heard. The country that he has visited or the symphony that he has heard, he knows not only intellectually but by experience. The Truth that we have demonstrated we are experiencing, for realization is experience. We all know *of* many spiritual truths that we have not yet been able to demonstrate. For instance, we know intellectually that our bodies are spiritual and perfect, and most of us have had some remarkable healings resulting from this knowledge, but not one of us has yet realized it completely, or even in a very high degree. We know, intellectually, that we dwell in eternity, but we are all still under the time-belief limitation, and have to respect it for the time being. We all know *intellectually* that we are one with God, but no one as yet is entirely free from fear and doubt, as he will be when realization comes. All these are truths that we know *of* but have only partially demonstrated; and of course there are others.

But we all know, too, that in God's universe there exist infinite spiritual ideas, infinite glories, of which we cannot begin to have the faintest notion at present. To understand more and more of these wondrous truths is our work for eternity.

In the verse which we are considering, "dry land" means the Truth that we have actually demonstrated, and therefore experienced. We saw above that realization and demonstration are one. This means that as soon as one realizes the spiritual truth concerning any difficulty or any lack, that difficulty will certainly be overcome or the lack supplied. Sometimes there is a time lag, or delay, between the realization and the appearance of the solution; but the time lag is never very long. Very often the realization is in the subconscious mind only, and then we are not yet consciously aware that the work has been finished. When we pray or treat we naturally expect that God will act (or otherwise it would be a bogus treatment), but in such a case we have no conscious assurance that the work has been done until the result appears in the outer.

Sometimes the realization reaches into the conscious mind as well as the subconscious, and then we get a wonderful sense of peace and satisfaction—the Dove Alights—and we know that the problem is solved, before the solution appears. It sometimes happens even after the dove has alighted that the condition seems to get worse for a time; but because the dove has come to you, and whispered the Truth, you know that all will be well—and it always is. In such cases it will be found that when the morning dawns everything concerning that situation will be far better than it was before the crisis arose (before evening fell), and then you will be glad, or your patient will be glad, that the difficulty did arise, because of the great advance in understanding that it has enabled you or him to make.

Technically, the change in your consciousness is the "demonstration," and the change seen in the outer picture is called the "sign," a word familiar to us in the gospels.

The waters and seas mentioned in the text stand for all Truth or all spiritual ideas that the individual has not yet demonstrated. These words include the ideas he knows *of*, and also the infinite ideas concerning which he knows nothing yet save that myriads of still unknown glories do exist. More particularly, the word "seas" applies to the spiritual truths that he does know *of*.

*And God said, Let the earth bring forth grass, the herb yield-
ing seed, and the fruit tree yielding fruit after his kind, whose
seed is in itself, upon the earth: and it was so.*

*And the earth brought forth grass, and herb yielding seed
after his kind, and the tree yielding fruit, whose seed was in itself, after his kind: and God saw that it was good.*

And the evening and the morning were the third day. (Genesis 1:11–13)

At this stage we see that man has begun to pray, because he now knows that God exists, and he has some
sense, however feeble, of the power and goodness of
God. He has accepted the fact that all that he seems to experience is not *true;* that the good is true and real, and
that the evil is temporary and can be destroyed when
one knows how. Even this knowledge, meager as it may
seem, revolutionizes his life. It shakes the edifice of error
as an earthquake shakes a flimsy building. A tremendous
amount of fear and doubt evaporates from his subconscious, and *healing begins to make its appearance.*

The condition that he is healing begins to improve.
This improvement at first seems to be small, but any
change means the beginning of the end; and small as it
is, it stimulates his faith.

All this is described in the text as the appearance of
vegetable life on the dry land. Vegetable life is indeed
life, but life in quite a limited form. Growing things can
develop where they are planted, but they cannot move
over the surface of the earth, they are rooted, tied down;
nor have they anything comparable to the degree of consciousness that even the lowest forms of true animal life
possess. When the dry land was definitely separated from
the water it was all ready to bear life, but was still actually barren; and now vegetable life appears. The Christ

within knows that freedom is coming, and rejoices—God sees that it is good.

Fourth Day

And God said, Let there be lights in the firmament of the heaven to divide the day from the night; and let them be for signs and for seasons, and for days, and years:

And let them be for lights in the firmament of heaven to give light upon the earth: and it was so.

And God made two great lights; the greater light to rule the day, and the lesser light to rule the night: he made the stars also.

And God set them in the firmament of the heaven to give light upon the earth.

And to rule over the day and over the night, and to divide the light from the darkness: and God saw that it was good.

And the evening and the morning were the fourth day. (Genesis 1:14–19)

As the demonstration grows, with the lessening of fear, man relies more and more clearly on the Truth of Being. He realizes, especially, that he is not doing the work himself as a limited personality, and that he never could do it in that way. He sees that his own efforts (relying upon his own intellect and his own will) cannot accomplish anything for him, that, in fact, he must get outside help. Only a very foolish person would try to pray to himself. That is why, at this stage, the Bible text leaves the earth and goes outside of it to the heavenly bodies.

So man now works to increase his understanding of God. We know that there are Seven Main Aspects of God, knowable by mankind in its present degree of development, and of these, Life, Truth, and Love are primary.[4] Life is being or existence in itself, and, for the practical purpose of healing, which after all is but the effort to know Life more correctly, Truth and Love are the more generally important aspects. They are referred to in this text as the greater and the lesser lights. Which is the greater and which the lesser light depends usually upon the individual. Some people have developed the understanding of the Truth or Intelligence side of Life more than the Love side, and for them it is more powerful, and is the greater light. Others have developed the understanding of the Love of God more than the Intelligence or Truth side of His nature, and for them Divine Love is the greater light. Note that Intelligence is especially an expression of Truth, and may be thought of as Truth in action.

As time goes on, we should, of course, seek to develop our understanding of both of these aspects equally, and when we have done so we shall have perfect wisdom, for wisdom is the correct balance of Intelligence and Love, and is therefore a compound quality. Faith (not blind belief, but understanding faith) may be thought of as wisdom in action.

The difference between the greater light and the lesser light sometimes shows itself better in the healing of a particular difficulty. One problem may call for the realization of Truth and Intelligence rather than of Love, irrespective of which the healer himself may have developed more. Where much fear or anger has to be met one should always try to realize Divine Love. Where there seems to be confusion, misunderstanding, or stupidity, Truth and Intelligence should be realized.

---

4. See chapter, "The Seven Main Aspects of God."

"Night" in the Bible, often means what we call today the subconscious mind. We saw above that we need to develop whichever wing of life is weaker in us—Love or Intelligence—until it is as strong as the other wing, and as we progress in this work we shall clear up the subconscious at a tremendous rate, which is to say, we shall rapidly develop wisdom.

Wisdom is the key to harmony in life, because wise thinking, producing wise words and wise deeds, can result only in good; and since, as we have seen, faith may be thought of as dynamic wisdom, or wisdom in action, we can see that faith is the secret of life, because according to your faith is it always done unto you.

This truth that Wisdom and Faith are the static and dynamic aspects of the same thing will repay careful consideration.

He made the stars also. Man views the physical stars with wonder and awe, but even today he knows little about them. Yet, just to see them, as mere points of light, is a matchless source of inspiration and encouragement. So, in the text, the stars stand for those glorious spiritual truths which we have dimly glimpsed, but of which we have little or no understanding so far. We know, in a vague and general way, that such truths exist. We catch some of their beauty, but at present that is all. Their importance to us lies in the wider outlook and the inspirational stimulus which they afford us.

The lights in the firmament thus symbolize the growth in our understanding, for in the Scriptures light is a common symbol for Truth, as darkness is for error.

In the Bible, as a rule, each figure carries several distinct but supplementary meanings. Thus those "lights" not only give us more understanding; they also teach us

the definite lesson of *order.* "Order is heaven's first law."[5]
Our spiritual work as well as our material activities should
be conducted in a regular and orderly manner. The seasons, the days, and the years refer to the orderly way in
which nature unfolds before our eyes—*for signs, and for
seasons, and for days, and for years.* The "signs" here referred to are the signs of the Zodiac.[6]

The reader is doubtless aware that all through the Bible
"the earth" stands for manifestation or expression, and
means your body, your home, your business, and your
surroundings in general.

Fifth Day

*And God said, Let the waters bring forth abundantly the mov-
ing creature that hath life, and fowl that may fly above the earth
in the open firmament of heaven.*

*And God created great whales, and every living creature that
moveth, which the waters brought forth abundantly, after their
kind, and every winged fowl after his kind: and God saw that
it was good.*

*And God blessed them, saying, Be fruitful, and multiply, and
fill the waters in the seas, and let fowl multiply in the earth.*

And the evening and the morning were the fifth day. (Genesis 1:20–23)

Here self-conscious moving creatures first make their
appearance. The restricted life of the vegetable kingdom
gives place to the much freer and more far-reaching existence of fishes and birds—moving creatures, as the text
calls them. The lives of these creatures, and the types of

---

5. Milton.
6. See chapter, "The Zodiac and the Bible."

experience enjoyed by them, however limited they may seem to us, are a tremendous advance upon those of the trees and plants, as a little thought will show.

Hebrew scholars tell us that a very remarkable word is here used for the first time in the original—the word *nephesh*. This word implies self-conscious life, and therefore it is not used in connection with the vegetable life which appeared on the third day. Now the word *nephesh* is complex in meaning, and includes the idea of inspiration, and the idea of fire which we know has always been, from the earliest times, a symbol for spirit—for that which is divine and eternal. The Old Testament people thought of the blood as being the vehicle of *nephesh*, and for this reason the Bible frequently uses blood as a symbol for *nephesh*. In the story of the murder of Abel, for instance,[7] God is represented as saying "The voice of thy brother's *blood* crieth unto me." Again, in the story of the exodus (Chapter 12), the *blood* is sprinkled upon the lintel and sides of the doors to protect the Israelites from the destroying angel. Elsewhere the Bible says "The blood is the life." In the New Testament, the blood of Jesus is used to symbolize the spirit and power of the Truth he taught. This implies that it is prayer, or the realization in some degree of spiritual truth, that saves us in the hour of danger. The lintel of the door is, of course, the entrance of the house (the consciousness) where error must be met and excluded.

Fishes and birds have self-consciousness and the power of locomotion. They can move about and change their environment.

All this symbolizes the idea that man's understanding is becoming really alive and powerful. He has actively

---

7. Genesis 4:10.

changed his thought for the better. The truth is much more vivid to him. This is the result of his having realized that only God can bring about good and that he himself can do nothing without God. As we have seen, it was only after the heavenly bodies or luminaries appeared that *nephesh* was introduced, and we had the fishes and birds. The treatment is now stirring powerfully and the demonstration moves rapidly forward.

Sixth Day

And God said, Let the earth bring forth the living creature after his kind, cattle, and creeping thing, and beast of the earth after his kind: and it was so.

And God made the beast of the earth after his kind, and cattle after their kind, and every thing that creepeth upon the earth after his kind: and God saw that it was good. (Genesis 1:24–25)

The realization of the Presence of God is the secret of demonstration or salvation. We have to realize that in Truth God is present where the trouble seems to be. It is not enough to know that God in Himself is good. We have to recognize that goodness as being where, at first, we knew fear and disharmony. There is a stage in man's development, and a corresponding stage in every healing, where the goodness of God as a general fact is realized in some degree, but the error still seems very real also. The final step is to know (in thought, of course, the only place we can know it) the goodness of God where the error seems to be. In other words, in the idiom of the Bible, good must be brought out of the "sea" of the abstract, onto the "dry land" of definite, *concrete* good.

That, of course, is what all healing and, in fact, every kind of demonstration is; and so moving creatures now appear on the dry land. Fishes and other marine creatures live immersed in the waters more or less remote from us. The birds fly over our heads in the air, also out of our reach—the fifth day stage—but the beasts of the earth, or as we might say, mammals, reptiles, and smaller creeping things, belong to the solid earth, and are easily within our reach. Here is another major advance. Some of these creatures are much higher than others in the scale of life, but in addition to possessing self-consciousness and locomotion they are all firmly established on the dry land too, not fixed to it like the plants, but masters of it. Demonstration now is within reach, and we need only to realize our rights and privileges in order to grasp it.

Creation of Man

And God said, Let us make man in our image, after our likeness: and let them have dominion over the fish of the sea, and over the fowl of the air, and over the cattle, and over all the earth, and over every creeping thing that creepeth upon the earth.

So God created man in His own image, in the image of God created He him; male and female created He them. (Genesis 1:26-27)

Now we reach the place in this wonderful allegory where man himself appears. Man has self-consciousness and locomotion, like the lower creatures, but in addition to this he has the divine qualities of intuition and reason, and *he can form a concept;* and these faculties put him in a class by himself. An animal knows particular things only. An intelligent dog, for instance, knows your house and my house, and various other houses which he has visited; but he cannot conceive of *a* house in a general sense—only some particular house. A man can think that a house should always have a porch, or that houses in general should have central heating; without having any special house in mind. These faculties—intuition, reason, the ability to form a concept—constitute his "dominion." They give him power over the lower creations, or power to make his demonstration.

You will notice that three, and only three, acts of creation are mentioned in this treatise:

The first is in verse 1, where the creation of the universe in general is mentioned.

The second is in verse 21, and refers to the coming into action of *nephesh* on the fifth day.

The third is in verse 27, when man first appears.

These are all capital steps in the unfoldment of Truth. In your treatment, the creation of man symbolizes your complete realization. Fear has gone. Your consciousness is now clear, and you know that the demonstration is certain to appear, if it has not already done so. Now, for the time being at least, you express your divine nature as nearly as you have ever done; and you know that you have dominion in your life, and that you have nothing to fear. You not only know the Truth, but you feel it. Now, at last, knowledge and feeling are balanced—"male and female created He them." In the Scriptures, the male always represents intellect and knowledge; and the female stands for the feeling nature.

Here I must explain that in Bible idiom the word "God" does not always stand for God in the sense of the Universal Creator. It may mean your own Indwelling Christ, or True Self, which, of course, is the Presence of God at the point where you are, for in your True Self you are an individualization of God. In like manner, the word "man" as in verse 27 and elsewhere, may stand for manifestation or what is in other verses of the Bible called the "earth." The divine spark, or the Presence of God in you (your true self) has now made your manifestation into His image and likeness, and the healing is accomplished. All this is equally true when you are healing someone else, for your patient is part of your manifestation, for the time being, since you must be either believing him to be sick or knowing him to be well.

And God blessed them, and God said unto them, Be fruitful and multiply, and replenish the earth, and subdue it: and have dominion over the fish of the sea, and over the fowl of the air, and over every living thing that moveth upon the earth. (Genesis 1:28)

Here the Bible further stresses the fact that man is to have dominion over his body and conditions. He is to be king in the world of his own manifestation. *Be fruitful and multiply, and replenish the earth, and subdue it,* means just that. To be fruitful, and multiply, is to grow in understanding and spiritual power, constantly to become aware of new ideas and to exploit them for God, and to do it through all eternity.

The universe in which we live is a universe of thought. It seems to be substantial, and to be separate from ourselves; just as the experiences of a dream seem to be; but, nevertheless, students of metaphysics know that it is really nothing but thought. Truly, that which we experience is nothing but our own thoughts and beliefs objectified. In technical language we say that "your own concept is what you see."

When most people hear this Truth for the first time it is hard for them to believe it, but careful thought and prayerful consideration in the end convinces them. Some

[handwritten margin notes:] Yet only God can change these thought for us, we cannot do it of ourselves, since ourselves, as we know them, are these thoughts. We must surrender our will to this, if our thoughts are to change. This is why only acts, in surrendering can change our thoughts. Our own thinking cannot do it.

people seem to know this Truth intuitively, even when they are very young, without it ever being told to them. Naturally, children never think in this logical manner, nor have they the vocabulary to correspond with it, but some children, in their own way, feel that the events of the outer world are not really what the grownup people pretend they are, but resemble rather one of their own games; or perhaps the Christmas play in which they took part at school—interesting and important in a way, but still not a real thing. When they seek further enlightenment on this subject from their elders, they naturally fail to make themselves understood. They are thought to be too imaginative and precocious, and are discouraged for their own good. In most cases this causes the knowledge finally to be forgotten.

When we learn to control our thinking we shall control our lives. We can have no control over our lives until we do succeed in controlling our thinking. Once more let it be said that we have to train ourselves, first to believe, and then to realize, the Presence of God where any negative condition seems to be. (Judge not according to the appearance, but judge righteous judgment.[8])

Different people will accomplish this in different ways, depending upon the temperament and outlook of the individual. In all cases you should claim frequently that God thinks through you, that God is inspiring you to use right methods, and that Divine Wisdom will show you the next step.

Above all, you must avoid being tense. The commonest mistake that people make is *to try too hard*. Never forget that in all mental working, effort defeats itself. Claim that Divine Spirit is praying through you, and believe it;

But this control comes only by submitting our thinking & our will to God. —Through action in surrender to His will.

---

8. John 7:24.

then you will not feel that desire to press hard, which is really will power. Praying in this way, your prayers will be answered much sooner.

Spiritual consciousness is continually "replenishing" its earth. We must never try to hold on, mentally, to present conditions or particular objects. As long as such things belong to us by right of consciousness they will stay, and nothing can separate them from us. If they go, it is really because we have outgrown them, and something better is coming. Let them go freely and without regret, for until they are gone the better thing cannot make its appearance.

AA
Acceptance
"Let go, +
Let God"

There is no such thing in the spiritual life as reaching a state of finality or completeness, a condition where everything is perfect, finished, and unchangeable. You never can reach a place where you may stop praying and, so to speak, rest upon your laurels. Such a condition would really mean that you had reached a point where you could stop communing with God. The "static" heaven of orthodoxy was often represented as something like this, but such an idea is fundamentally wrong. To cease our communion with God would in itself be to slip out of heaven, and back into limitation. As long as we do maintain our living communion with God our consciousness will grow and grow, and our individual manifestation will naturally be expanded and enriched in proportion. A man said resentfully, "Am I to go on working forever?" That clearly showed a fundamental misunderstanding. Working, in the sense of toil or drudgery, is not spiritual communion at all, and does not lead us into heaven. The prayer or treatment that does bring us into heaven produces a sense of joyous fellowship with God, and is the very reverse of drudgery.

Truth students frequently use the word "working" when they mean praying or treating. They say "I worked for such a thing," or, "you should work in such a way." This term is a convenient one, as long as we understand that it does not imply a task or an arduous activity.

The fish, the fowl, and the beasts of the earth represent in detail different qualities and powers that belong to the spiritual man. The human being, as we know him now, possesses all these things, but only in germ, as the oak tree exists potentially in the acorn, and he will gradually develop them as he progresses spiritually. The completion of this development will be his dominion over the fish, the fowl, and the animals on the earth.

And God said, Behold, I have given you every herb bearing seed, which is upon the face of all the earth, and every tree, in the which is the fruit of a tree yielding seed; to you it shall be for meat.

And to every beast of the earth, and to every fowl of the air, and to every thing that creepeth upon the earth, wherein there is life, I have given every green herb for meat: and it was so. (Genesis 1:29–30)

God works in and through His creation at all times. In truth God is the only power—the only Cause. When God inspires us to do something He, at the same time, furnishes everything that we need with which to do it, and He furnishes the power wherewith it is done. "Who goeth a warfare any time at his own charges?"[9]

Here the vegetable kingdom represents this provision. It stands for everything that we can need in order to do God's work, which means, of course, to express Him. It includes any material equipment of any kind, any introductions or cooperation that we may need, any financial support, and, above all, any information, new ideas, clearer understanding, guidance or wisdom; as well as the necessary energy to put any enterprise through. Such

---

9. 1 Corinthians 9:7.

things may be thought of as the food or "meat" of the undertaking, and it is in that sense the text uses this word in verses 29 and 30.

It is an ancient maxim that everything directly or indirectly comes out of the ground originally, and we see that the Scripture with divine logic begins by stating the existence of God's unfailing provision in making the vegetable creation appear as soon as the dry earth is available, and before any of the higher and more intricate creations arrive.

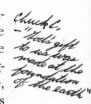

It is a universal rule, as we all know, that living things produce offspring after their own kind. Thoughts are living things. Indeed they are particularly vital living things, and so thoughts naturally follow this law. Positive thoughts produce positive, harmonious conditions; and negative thoughts produce fear and limitation. The Bible is never tired of stating this law, and expounding it with example after example, from Genesis to Revelation; and we must never get tired of reminding ourselves of it, in season and out of season. It is interesting to note that the characteristic color of the vegetable kingdom when it is healthy, is green, and that is spiritual symbolism, the color green stands for Intelligence. It is this aspect of God—Intelligence—expressed in the individual as an intelligent understanding of Divine Law—especially this particular law which is of such vital importance for us—that is the basis of all consistent and reliable demonstration, as distinct from occasional and sporadic answers to prayer. Therefore this law already begins to be revealed in the dry land or third day phase, when vegetation makes its appearance.

And God saw every thing that he had made, and, behold, it was very good, and the evening and the morning were the sixth day. (Genesis 1:31)

In describing each stage of creation the Bible tells us significantly that God sees that His creation is good. No condemnation or regret is expressed anywhere. Creation is revealed as definitely good. Life is good. Life is a blessing. Life is a glorious gift, and a sublime opportunity. That is the Bible teaching about life—*that it is good*.

The Scriptures recognize the temporary existence of evil and suffering, but they teach that such things are not real in the sense of being substantial and therefore permanent. They teach that we bring these things upon ourselves by our own wrong thinking and false beliefs. This wrong thinking includes not only sin but the harboring of false beliefs of any kind, which means lack of correct knowledge of life. They teach that we become free from suffering and limitation, and attain to glorious happiness, by studying the laws of God and then living in accordance with them.

AA

step 3 "our troubles, we think, are basically of our own making. They arise out of ourselves."

Thus the religion of the Bible is diametrically opposed to that of some of the Eastern philosophies which are essentially pessimistic. Those philosophies postulate the life of man, self-conscious existence, as an evil in itself. For them life is essentially a misfortune, necessarily filled with suffering and disappointment, and it is for us to get rid of it as soon as we possibly can. Self-conscious existence, they teach, is a curse; and man's only hope is to kill out all interest in life and ultimately to cease to have conscious being.

Not the way Baba sees it. — But this is the way some "fundamentalist" Christians seem to see it.

Western students who embrace such a philosophy seldom realize its true import. They are attracted to it by the kindly, blameless lives that so many of its votaries lead. The teaching of mercy and brotherhood that accompanies this philosophy must command our sincere admiration; but the fact remains that fundamentally it is pessimism, the

Is this really true in the original inspiration of such philosophies — or only in the orthodoxies that they rigidified into? — The way the original inspiration was rigidified into + reduced an the orthodoxy + establishment?

Or is it really a new dimension or aspect or degree of the truth revealed by Christ, not given in earlier revelation? — although this is earlier than Christ + this is in Old Testament

advocacy of spiritual suicide (if such a thing were possible). Others adopt it because its great simplicity is restful and soothing to minds and hearts confused and wearied by the complicated and artificial theologies of Christian orthodoxy.

It should be clearly understood that you will never lose your individuality. Ultimately, when you attain full conscious union with God, and *know* that you are one with Him, you will still know yourself as an individual, and you will maintain that identity through all eternity. You will always be growing and developing, but you will always be you. By that time you will have forgotten the worries and griefs that you will have left behind you in the past, just as an adult forgets most of the griefs and fears of infancy, and even many of the recent past. Complete conscious union with God does not mean absorption and annihilation of individuality.

Baba also says this.

Man, in his realization of God, is not in the least like a drop of water falling back into the ocean, as one poet thought; for such a drop of water is distributed and lost in the ocean—ceases to exist as that drop. Man may be likened to a spark thrown out by a blazing fire. The spark, from a tiny beginning, develops into a great blaze, a living fire—not indeed one and the same as the parent fire, but utterly one with it, because all fire is fire.

Baba seems to agree with [...] — the drop is not lost, but grows to include or become conscious of the whole ocean.

Seventh Day

Thus the heavens and the earth were finished, and all the host of them.

And on the seventh day God ended his work which he had made; and he rested on the seventh day from all his work which he had made.

And God blessed the seventh day, and sanctified it: because that in it he had rested from all his work which God created and made. (Genesis 2:1–3)

You pray or treat about a certain subject until you obtain a vivid realization concerning it. When you have reached this point you do not feel any need or inclination to pray further on that matter. You are satisfied, and with a deep and indescribable satisfaction and certitude. This is the *Seventh Day*, when you rest, with a feeling of praise and thanksgiving.

It often happens that you do not actually obtain a good realization, and yet you feel that you have done all you can, at least for the time being. To go on working beyond this point would be to use will power, and so you bless the work that you have done, and leave it. You have spoken the Word. You have voiced the Truth. As a witness for God you have testified for His omnipresence unaltered and unalterable; and now comes the rest unto the people of God—having done all to stand. In such a case the demonstration is usually made, and then the sign itself is the Seventh Day.

In the history of a particular demonstration, the "Seven Days" may actually occupy a long or a short time in the calendar or on the clock. One problem may be solved in a week, another in a few hours, or even minutes. Some glorious demonstrations have taken many years as we count time; but in each case these seven stages were gone through. The individual stages were longer or shorter in different cases, and the Seventh Day came sometimes only with the appearance of the sign, as we have seen, and sometimes beforehand. In the beautiful experience that we call an instantaneous demonstration, the seven stages are still traversed, but so rapidly that we are not aware of them. Nevertheless, the work is done in the order explained, for that is the way in which the human mind works out of limitation, under the action of God.

This, then, is the story told by the first chapter of Genesis; simple, yet all-embracing, for these thirty-four verses are nothing less than the life history of humanity, and at the same time they furnish a road map to salvation and to eternity. Wisely does the Bible begin with this revelation, for it is indeed the gateway of Heaven.

Adam and Eve

T HE story of Adam and Eve in the Garden of Eden is the greatest parable in the Bible. It is supremely important because it explains the real nature of our life here on earth. It tells us about ourselves and how we bring about the conditions in which we live. It is the textbook on spiritual and psychological anatomy. When you thoroughly understand the Garden of Eden story you will understand human nature, and when you understand human nature, you will have dominion over it. This parable is placed almost at the beginning of the Bible because it is the foundation upon which the whole of the Bible is built; and all the rest of the Bible, to the end of Revelation, assumes an understanding of the Garden of Eden parable. Indeed, there is only one Bible section in front of it, and that is the basic first chapter which gives the fundamentals of spiritual demonstration.

The Bible is not primarily intended to teach history, or biography, or natural science. It is intended to teach psychology and metaphysics. It deals primarily with states

of mind and the laws of mental activity; and anything
else is only incidental. Each of the principal characters in
the Bible represents a state of mind that any of us may experience; and the events that happen to the various characters illustrate the consequences to us of entertaining
such states of mind, either good or bad.

Some of the Bible characters, such as Moses, Elijah,
and Paul, are historical figures. They were real men who
lived on earth and did the deeds attributed to them;
nonetheless they represent states of mind also, and, of
course, they outpictured different states of mind at different times as their lives unfolded. Other Bible characters, such as Adam and Eve, the Prodigal Son, the Good
Samaritan,[1] or the Scarlet Woman[2] are, of course, fic-
tional and never had an actual existence; but they express states of mind too, and always in a remarkably simple
and graphic manner.

Now a state of mind cannot be viewed or pictured directly as can a material object. It can only be described
indirectly, by a figure of speech, an allegory, or a parable, but, unfortunately, thoughtless people have always
tended to take the figure of speech or the allegory literally, at its face value, thus missing the real meaning,
because it lies hidden beneath. The veil of Isis comes to
be worshipped while Isis herself is forgotten. Another
evil that follows from this course is that, since many parables obviously *cannot* be literally true, such people, unable to accept the authenticity of the story, proceed to
reject the Bible altogether as a collection of falsehoods.
This was the attitude of Ingersoll in America, Bradlaugh
in England, and many others. The fundamentalist, on the

---

1. Luke 10:33.
2. Revelation 17:3–4.

other hand, does violence to his common sense in trying to make himself believe that these parables are literally true, while at the bottom of his heart—which is
the place that matters—he cannot really believe them,
and so a dangerous conflict is set up within his subconscious.

You cannot take a pencil and draw a picture of fear
for instance; but you can draw a picture of a human
being, and depict terror on his countenance. You cannot take a brush and paint remorse, or envy, or sensuality as such; but you can take a pen and write about a great
fire, and about a soul suffering torment in the flames,
and then you will have an excellent description of the
suffering brought about by these evils. Yet, many people
are certain to think that you mean an actual human body
being burned in a physical fire. You cannot picture a soul
experiencing a sense of perfect peace and harmony, but
you can speak of an expert musician playing beautiful
music upon a perfectly tuned harp; and again many people will think that the redeemed soul is to spend eternity literally playing a harp. Justice is an abstract quality
that cannot be drawn or sculptured, but you can draw
or sculpture a woman, blindfolded, and holding a balance in her hand; and when you do that we all know that
you mean justice. So the Bible uses this method to im-
part its teaching. It uses outer concrete things to express
inner, subjective or abstract ideas. As Paul says, these
things are an allegory.

In the Garden of Eden story many people seem to
think that Eve symbolizes woman as a sex and that Adam
somehow stands for man as a sex, but this is absurd. Adam
and Eve represent one person. They represent Every-
man. They represent you and me and every other man
and woman on the globe. They stand for the human

being as we know him. *Adam means the body,* and *Eve means the soul or human mind,* which consists of the intellect and the feeling nature. In the Bible, woman always means the soul.

The story says that Eve ate a certain fruit, and that as a result of eating it she and Adam were turned out of Paradise, and incurred all the pains and sorrows that human nature knows. This is the great parable because it lays down the Great Law at one stroke. The fact is that the body cannot experience anything that does not first appear in the mind; and the mind cannot entertain any conviction without its effect appearing upon the body or embodiment. So it is not by chance that the fatal fruit was first eaten by Eve and not by Adam. The body cannot do anything to the soul because the body is effect and not cause. The body is a shadow cast by the mind, and the shadow cannot do anything to affect the object by which it is cast.

Baba

At this point you should note carefully that the word "body" means the complete embodiment of the subject, and includes not only his physical body but all his material surroundings of every kind. The Great Law of human nature is that one's surroundings at any time are but the outer expression or outpicturing of his conscious (and subconscious) mind at the moment. States of mind never result from outer conditions (although, of course, they *seem* to do so until we analyze the situation thoroughly), but it is always the outer picture which is produced by the mental state. Eve can bring trouble upon Adam or she can present him with harmony; but Adam cannot do anything to Eve. Unless the soul first eats the forbidden fruit of fear, anger, greed, etc., the embodiment will be harmonious and free; but anything that the soul does consume or entertain must and will appear on the body.

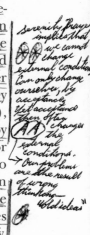

This is the essential significance of the Garden of Eden parable, and we will now consider the details in logical order, at some length. Every one of these details is extremely important and instructive. Each one of them gives us an important clue to our own nature, but they are still secondary to the great central theme that *this is a mental universe*, and that it is the mind that produces all phenomena.

I recommend that the reader carefully reread the Book of Genesis, Chapters 2 and 3, beginning at Chapter 2, Verse 4, and using the Authorized or King James Version, which is the one in general use. It will be noticed that the first three verses of Chapter 2 as printed in our Bible, really belong to Chapter 1, and are not part of the Adam and Eve parable. The Bible was not divided into chapters and verses until late in the Christian era. The original authors knew nothing of this arrangement, but it is a very convenient one although in certain cases the divisions have not been made in the right place.

The first point that we have to note is the nature of the fruit that Eve ate. It is the fruit of the tree of the knowledge of good and evil (Genesis 2:17). Note this very carefully. What kind of tree is specified? It is the tree of the knowledge of good and evil; and so the meaning is obviously allegorical. No such tree grows literally on the earth. This point proves beyond question that *the story is an allegory* and is meant to be taken as such. There seems to be a popular belief that it was an apple that Eve ate, but the Bible knows nothing about this. What she ate was the fruit of the tree of the knowledge of good and evil. How people could ever have taken this wonderful allegory for historical fact it is hard to see, but such has happened, and all the orthodox theologies are founded upon a supposed "fall of man" caused by literally eating the fruit of an actual tree in an authentic geographical location, at a definite date in the past—yet the whole thing is clearly pure allegory, like the story of the Good Samaritan, or one of Aesop's fables, except that it teaches far greater and deeper lessons. A very little thought will show that to create an adult human pair, totally inexperienced through having no youth or childhood behind them, and then punish them for a transgression, the nature of which they could not possibly understand, would not be intelligent; and how much more unintelligent and unjust to mete out disabilities and punishments to their distant posterity for an event which took place centuries before they were born, and for which they were in no way responsible.

The account says:

"And the Lord God commanded the man, saying, Of every tree of the garden thou mayest freely eat: But of the tree of the knowledge of good and evil, thou shalt not eat of it: for in the day that thou eatest thereof thou shalt surely die." (Genesis 2:16–17)

This clearly means that if we indulge in the knowledge of both good and evil we will suffer; that is to say, if we entertain both good and evil thoughts, trouble will come to us. It does not say that this will happen if we eat fruit which is entirely evil, which means holding thoughts that are entirely negative, for no one in his senses would do that. The trouble lies in the *mixed fruit*. It is the mixture of good and evil in our thinking that brings about our downfall. When people think evil, the carnal mind always furnishes what seems to be a good reason for it. When people criticize others, when they entertain thoughts of resentment and condemnation, when they fill their minds with thoughts of sickness, lack, and so forth, they are very apt to invent seemingly good reasons for

The Pale Horseman ?

so doing and thereby deceive themselves, thus eating mixed fruit. The law is that we must not think evil under any circumstances or we will suffer the consequences.

Man has free will to think good or evil and he constantly chooses to think evil, and it is this evil thinking that is the "fall of man." Thus the fall of man is going on all the time, whenever we allow ourselves to think wrongly. It is not an event in the past but a constant occurrence, and it is to be overcome by training ourselves to think rightly at all times.

In the Adam and Eve story the male makes his appearance first, because the human being is always aware of his body long before he discovers his soul. This is true of mankind as a race, and is also true of the individual in babyhood.

"Now the serpent was more subtle than any beast of the field which the Lord God had made. And he said unto the woman, Yea, hath God said, Ye shall not eat of every tree of the garden?

"And the woman said unto the serpent, We may eat of the fruit of the trees of the garden:

"But of the fruit of the tree which is in the midst of the garden, God hath said, Ye shall not eat of it, neither shall ye touch it, lest ye die.

"And the serpent said unto the woman, Ye shall not surely die." (Genesis 3:1–4)

The serpent represents the lower nature. It stands for the carnal mind. The carnal mind, an expression which we owe to Paul, is the belief that we are separate from God, whereas in reality we are one with Him. It is the belief that inner things are subservient to outer things, instead of the reverse, or that there is power in matter. This mistaken belief is well called the "fall of man," for it is the cause of all our problems and difficulties. That belief is an extremely subtle one. We all know only too well how easily it creeps into our thinking, without our being aware of it. We accept the Jesus Christ teaching; we think we understand it; and yet we constantly catch ourselves forgetting it at important times. Such error is therefore very well depicted as a serpent or snake, which, with its silent, subtle movement, strikes its victim without warning.

trick of the ego

The world thinks that by analyzing evil, studying it, filling our minds with it, we shall obtain power over it. It says, with the serpent:

"For God doth know that in the day ye eat thereof, then your eyes shall be opened, and ye shall be as gods, knowing good and evil." (Genesis 3:5)

Of course, the opposite is the truth. The only way to overcome evil is to refuse to touch it mentally—or, if we have already done so, to un-know it.

The great parable goes on to say that when the couple had eaten this fruit they realized that they were naked and they were afraid. As soon as we allow evil to obtain a hold on our minds, fear grips us and we feel unprotected or "naked" in that sense, and we look about for some material thing to save us—whereas our only salvation is to know that evil is not real. Before eating the forbidden fruit, Adam and Eve were not conscious of being unprotected or naked.

The parable goes on to explain that in the cool of the day they heard the voice of God challenging them. This means that after the harm has been done, when we have entertained negative thoughts and begun to suffer the consequences we have time to reflect, and then we turn to God and wonder what He will think or do about it.

Of course, Eve tempts Adam, and Adam blames Eve because, as we have seen, nothing can happen to the body that does not first find itself in the soul. You may say that something has happened to your body that you knew nothing about previously, but there must have been a corresponding thought or mental equivalent in your mind or the thing itself could not have happened to you. The explanation is that it was in the unconscious part of your mind and so you knew nothing about it, but nevertheless it was there.

"Therefore the Lord God sent him forth from the garden of Eden, to till the ground from whence he was taken." (Genesis 3:23)

Our belief in the reality of evil and limitation is the cause of all our troubles. It is the cause of sickness. It is the cause of quarrels and inharmony. It is the cause of poverty, for when we *know* the Truth of Being instead of only *believing* it, we shall not have to toil and drudge for a living, but our thought will be creative, and we shall demonstrate what we need. In the meantime, because Eve has eaten the forbidden fruit—because the race believes in limitation—we have to toil for a living. The earth has to be tilled with labor, and when the crops come up they seem to be subject to all kinds of pests and other dangers. "In the sweat of thy face shalt thou eat bread." (Genesis 3:19)

"Unto the woman he said, I will greatly multiply thy sorrow and thy conception; in sorrow thou shalt bring forth children; and thy desire shall be to thy husband, and he shall rule over thee." (Genesis 3:16)

As a result of the Fall—the belief in limitation—the soul produces new ideas with much labor and trouble. Artistic creations and new inventions come to the race slowly and with difficulty. The Egyptians could have had the telephone; the Romans could have had the automobile; if only they had known how, for nature was as ready to furnish them in those days as now. Even a century from today mankind will enjoy many blessings that we have to go without, because we have not yet discovered or invented them. The real, spiritual man, can have anything he needs at any moment by speaking the creative Word.

"So he drove out the man; and he placed at the east of the garden of Eden Cherubims, and a flaming sword which turned every way, to keep the way of the tree of life." (Genesis 3:24)

Eating the forbidden fruit—believing in limitation—is the fall of man, and by it we are driven out of Paradise and must remain outside until the false belief is relinquished. The law of harmony prevents the holder of a false belief from getting into Paradise, no matter from what direction he may try. For instance, as long as you believe that your body is material and limited and therefore subject to sickness and accident, you cannot have perfect health. When you *know* that your true body is spiritual and eternal, perfect health will come.

Adam and Eve represent the human being as we know him. This is not the real spiritual man who is perfect and eternal, but the person that we know here on this plane. Now, what is the human being? What is your human personality, for instance? It is your sincere opinion about yourself, or, to put it philosophically, it is your concept of yourself, that and nothing more. You are what you *really* believe yourself to be. You experience what you *really* believe in. All there is to any phenomenon is our belief in it. There is no difference between the thing and the thought of the thing. We often hear it said that thoughts are things, but the actual truth is that things are thoughts. From this it follows that when you "un-think" a thing it disappears. The world you live in is the world of your own beliefs. You created it by thinking it, and you can destroy it at any moment by un-thinking it. This is the meaning of the startling statement, "dust thou art, and unto dust thou shalt return." (Genesis 3:19)

Again I would impress upon the reader not to forget the subconscious mind. The subconscious mind (usually called in medical books, the unconscious) is that part of your mentality of which you are not aware. You may be unaware that you have been holding a certain thought or a certain belief, and yet it may be in your subconscious, and if so it will affect your life, in spite of the fact that you did not consciously know of its existence. You probably picked it up in childhood.

The importance of prayer lies in the fact that prayer, and prayer alone, can and does redeem and re-educate the subconscious.

Human belief is a temporary thing, always changing, falling into dust. Your real spiritual self *understands;* your temporary human self only *believes*. Understanding is of Truth and is therefore permanent. It is the "firmament" of Genesis 1:6. The first chapter of Genesis deals with the spiritual man and eternal Truth. This section, the second and third chapters, deals with man as we know him, or think we know him, for the time being.

"And I will put enmity between thee and the woman, and between thy seed and her seed; it shall bruise thy head, and thou shalt bruise his heel." (Genesis 3:15)

The enmity between the human soul and the serpent is easily understood, and here is a prophecy that mankind will ultimately overcome limitation and fear; that it shall bruise the head of the serpent. Meanwhile, until this happens, the serpent will continue to give man a good deal of trouble. The "heel" refers to whatever is the most vulnerable spot—this may be a love of money, a tendency to criticism

and condemnation, it may be sensuality, or anything else.
The heel has always been a symbol of man's weak spot,
for it is the place where he contacts the ground. The heel
of Achilles naturally comes to mind in this connection,
and see also Jacob's dying prophecy concerning Dan.[3]

When the Bible speaks of the "Lord," or as it does in
this section, of the "Lord God," it means *your concept* or
idea of God, and not necessarily God as He really is. For
instance, we are told elsewhere that the Lord hardened
Pharaoh's heart,[4] and this means that Pharaoh's own
(mistaken) idea of God hardened his heart, not that the
true God did this. We are sadly aware how often throughout Christian history the name of God has been invoked
by perfectly sincere people to justify religious persecution. Again, it was their false concept of God that led
them to do these cruel things and not, of course, the
true God Himself. When the true God is meant, the Bible
uses simply the word "God" or "Elohim," and of course
the words Life and Truth and Love are Aspects of God.[5]
John said "God is Love," and Jesus said, "I am the Way, the
Truth, and the Life."

In the Adam and Eve parable we find the term "Lord
God" employed, and so we are dealing with man's concept of God—which is the God he worships—and therefore the God which governs his life. It was Pharaoh's idea
of God, a despotic oriental sultan like himself, which
hardened his heart.

In the dialogue between the Lord God and Adam
and Eve, it is man's own consciousness that carries on

---

3. Genesis 49:17, and chapter, "The Four Horsemen of the
   Apocalypse."
4. Exodus 10:1.
5. See chapter, "The Seven Main Aspects of God."

a dialogue with itself, in exploring and analyzing the events that have happened. Who is there who has not carried on such a debate with himself, such an argument between the higher and the lower nature, in weighing the pros and cons of a particular temptation or a particular problem?

"Unto Adam also and to his wife did the Lord God make coats of skins, and clothed them." (Genesis 3:21)

Adam and Eve, having accepted the belief in limitation as a real thing to be grappled with, proceed to make themselves "coats of skins" thus endeavoring to correct one limitation belief with another limitation belief, and so getting deeper into confusion.

"And the Lord God said, Behold, the man is become as one of us, to know good and evil; and now, lest he put forth his hand, and take also of the tree of life, and eat, and live for ever." (Genesis 3:22)

They finally reach a condition of discouragement and doubt when they feel that there is no way out, that "what cannot be cured must be endured," and that sin, sickness, old age, and death are inevitable. This belief shuts them away from the tree of life. Otherwise they would have put forth their hands—they would have treated and overcome their negative thoughts—and taken of the fruit of the tree of life, eaten and lived forever. The tree of life is the *understanding* that we are one with God and that our true selves are spiritual and eternal. Such understanding is not mere intellectual doctrine, for it actually heals the body and ultimately regenerates it.

Jesus came to teach us about the tree of life and how to eat of its fruit, and thus overcome the fall of man. He said: "Seek ye first the kingdom of God, and all things shall be added unto you."[6] And he said: "The kingdom of

6. Matthew 6:33; Luke 12:31.

God is within you."[7] In the Bible the word "within" signifies thought, as distinct from the outer world of things.

"And a river went out of Eden to water the Garden;
and from thence it was parted, and became into four
heads.

"The name of the first is Pison: that is it which compasseth the whole land of Havilah, where there is gold;

"And the gold of that land is good: there is bdellium
and the onyx stone.

"And the name of the second river is Gihon: the same
is it that compasseth the whole land of Ethiopia.

"And the name of the third river is Hiddekel: that is it
which goeth toward the east of Assyria. And the fourth
river is Euphrates." (Genesis 2:10–14)

In connection with the parable of Adam and Eve, we
are told of a remarkable river that had its source in Eden,
but on flowing out of the garden divided itself into four
branches. This is a profound expression of the nature of
man. Man is one, a spiritual being, the expression of
God, perfect and eternal; but owing to his belief in limitation he seems for the time being to be divided up into
four parts, and this division only appears after the river
leaves Eden. We shall become very familiar with these
four divisions as the Bible goes on. They are spoken of as
the "Four Horsemen of the Apocalypse," as the "Four
Beasts around the throne," in the same Book of Revelation, and are mentioned in other parts of the Bible.[8]

There is no need to discuss them in detail here, and it
will suffice to say that the river Pison stands for man's spiritual nature—the White Horse. The land of Havilah
"where there is gold" is spiritual consciousness. Gold always

7. Luke 17:21.
8. See chapter, "The Four Horsemen of the Apocalypse."

stands for the truth that the power of God is present everywhere. Man often thinks that there is power and safety in money or material so-called security. He worships the golden calf, making a God of money, and thereby confusing the symbol with the truth that lies behind it. All religious movements have been in danger of mistaking the symbols of God for God Himself, and thus drifting into unconscious idolatry. The gold of Havilah is *good*, that is to say, it is the recognition of God Himself as the only power, and this recognition is the one thing that can never fail us. Pison in a special sense stands for God as Life, and bdellium and the onyx stone represent Truth and Love; the spiritual consciousness being essentially composed of Life, Truth, and Love. Pison is a reference to the river Indus which for the people of the Bible lay far to the east, and the East we know means inspiration and the Presence of God.[9]

The river Gihon represents the feeling nature or the Red Horse. It is a reference to the Nile and to Egypt which later became the land of bondage. Ethiopia was adjacent to ancient Egypt, and many people do in practice bring about most of their troubles or bondage through being unable to control the emotional nature.

The river Hiddekel stands for the intellect or the Black Horse. It is a reference to the Tigris and goes toward Assyria, which means will power; and we know that pure intellect has nothing but will power with which to express itself, and that will power always fails us in the end.

The fourth river, Euphrates, here stands for the body or matter, the Pale Horse. It is a remarkable fact that the Euphrates has constantly shifted its course even during historical times. Several different beds of the Euphrates,

9. See chapter, "The Four Horsemen of the Apocalypse."

formed during the last 2,000 years, have been traced out by geologists.[10] The instability of matter is known to every student of metaphysics, and is implied in this reference.

Notice that inside the Garden of Eden the river is one, and that it is only after leaving Paradise that it divides into four branches. When man regains his realization of his oneness with God, only his spiritual consciousness will remain, the lesser things having disappeared.

"And out of the ground the Lord God formed every beast of the field, and every fowl of the air; and brought them unto Adam to see what he would call them: and whatsoever Adam called every living creature, that was the name thereof." (Genesis 2:19)

We know that in the Bible the name of anything means its nature or character, and here we see that Adam's own beliefs and convictions led him to stamp each animal with a certain nature or opinion and that, having done so, the animal bore that character so far as he was concerned. We are affected, not by the real nature of things but by what we *think* is their real nature. What you have to live with is not *really* people and things in themselves but your idea of people and things. As we have said, in technical language, your own concept is what you see. You do not know the real Jones—all that you know is your idea of Jones, which may or may not be fairly correct. This is equally true of things. We know, for instance, that some people delight in very cold weather. It makes them feel well and happy, whereas others feel ill when the temperature is too low, and are mentally paralyzed by it. Also it should be carefully noticed that nothing can affect us unless it gets into our mentalities. A European in the

---

10. The Field Museum, Chicago, has an interesting relief map showing this.

middle of Africa is not injured by a local superstition that almost kills a native with fear, because the white man does not happen to believe in it. Of course, the white man has many superstitions of his own by which he is duly punished, and the African, who has never heard of them, is immune. This is the meaning of the saying in metaphysics that if you keep a thought out of your mentality it cannot affect you; but, as usual, you must remember that it can be in your subconscious without your knowing it. We have all received many negative suggestions in our childhood from well meaning people who said that we must avoid drafts, or we could not digest a certain dish, or that our lungs were very delicate, and so forth.

Buba

It is also true that good thoughts, such as thoughts of Divine Love, of health, and of success, cannot affect us if we keep them out of our mentalities; and so we ought to build in such thoughts industriously by daily prayer and meditation.

Sickness cannot affect you if your mentality contains a strong belief in health; and if you do not have such a belief, all the diets and exercises in the world cannot make you well or keep you alive.

If someone hates you it cannot have the slightest effect upon you as long as it is his hatred and not yours. But if there is hatred in *your* heart, that can do you unlimited harm according to its intensity. If you have what we call a prosperity consciousness you cannot experience poverty no matter what happens in the outer world; all the supply you need will come from *somewhere;* and if you have a poverty consciousness, prosperity will not stay with you, no matter what happens. It is notorious that people who gain large sums of money through gambling— whether by winning a sweepstake or through having

Because of the element of fear +/or self-pity.

broken the bank in a casino—lose their winnings before long, and do not get any happiness or permanent good from them. In the end we always express our consciousness, and the only way to improve things is to make the consciousness better.

An inventory helps us see where our consciousness has been flawed

"And the Lord God caused a deep sleep to fall upon Adam, and he slept: and he took one of his ribs, and closed up the flesh instead thereof;

"And the rib, which the Lord God had taken from man, made he a woman, and brought her unto the man.

"And Adam said, This is now bone of my bones, and flesh of my flesh: she shall be called Woman, because she was taken out of Man." (Genesis 2:21–23)

"And Adam called his wife's name Eve; because she was the mother of all living." (Genesis 3:20)

A deep sleep fell upon Adam and there is no mention in the Bible of his having reawakened, and indeed, our material lives are very little more than a dream of limitation, fear, and separation from God. "Awake thou that sleepest, and arise from the dead, and Christ shall give thee light."[11]

It is very interesting and significant to note that the word woman really means "one with" or "a part of" man, and emphasizes the fact that body and mind are one—that in fact the body is only the embodiment or outpicturing of the mind. Many philosophers have spoken of the body as a garment which the soul assumes, or a vehicle in which it travels, or as a vessel which contains it as a vase may contain water; but these similes are totally false. The body is no garment or independent vessel. It is the true picture of the soul or mentality. The body, if you like, is a shadow cast by the mind, copying it in every detail. Adam

---

11. Ephesians 5:14.

feels intuitively that he and the woman are one, and he calls her Eve because she is the mother of all that is—the mind is the sole creator.

"Therefore shall a man leave his father and his mother, and shall cleave unto his wife: and they shall be one flesh." (Genesis 2:24)

In the Bible, one's parents usually mean one's own past, because it is the common belief that our conditions today are caused by past events and that in this sense yesterday is the parent of today. When Jesus told the man not to go back to bury his father he was not, of course, suggesting that the duties and decencies of life should be neglected. He meant that that man was to stop thinking that he was limited by past mistakes. The man in question was probably burdened by some remorse or resentment concerning his past and was keeping himself out of the Kingdom in consequence. The lesson here is that the only thought we have to deal with is the present one, and that if we heal that we shall experience harmony; for yesterday has no power over today, unless we think it has.

Today's experience is caused only by today's thoughts and beliefs, and not by the thoughts or by the events or conditions of yesterday—appearances notwithstanding.

You are positively not in bondage to yesterday. Any bondage today can only come from today's bondage thoughts. Change today's thought and today's conditions must change to correspond, for Adam and Eve are one. Just as Adam represents the human being who is deceived by the serpent, so Jesus represents the Christ power which is the understanding of Truth that ultimately sets Adam free. When we suffer from a false belief it is the recognition of the Truth that liberates us. If you supposed yourself to be suffering from a serious malady you would experience all the fear and worry that could arise

from such a condition, but then if someone in whose
judgment you had confidence—say a physician of standing—told you that you were mistaken and that you did not
have any such complaint, all your fear and worry would
immediately go. Note that the physician would not have
cured the malady; he could not because you did not have
it; but he healed you of a false belief. The Christ Truth
does this.

"But now is Christ risen from the dead, and become the
firstfruits of them that slept.

"For since by man came death, by man came also the
resurrection of the dead.

"FOR AS IN ADAM ALL DIE, EVEN SO IN CHRIST
SHALL ALL BE MADE ALIVE.

"But every man in his own order: Christ the firstfruits;
afterward they that are Christ's at his coming.

"Then cometh the end, when he shall have delivered
up the kingdom of God, even the Father; when he shall
have put down all rule and all authority and power.

"For he must reign till he hath put all enemies under
his feet.

"The last enemy that shall be destroyed is death." (1
Corinthians 15:20–26)

You now understand that you are not a physical body
but a mentality, and as such you have certain beliefs and
a certain amount of understanding, and that what you
do is to outpicture the net result of all these beliefs and
that understanding. Such outpicturing constitutes your
body, your outer environment, and, in fact, all your experience. As time goes on your mentality improves or
declines according to the way you think, and the outer picture of your life changes in accordance with it.

Only prayer, the Christ power, can change things for the
better because nothing else really changes you. As long

AA
necessity of a
complete
psychic
change

as you remain the person that you are you must have the same sort of life that you have now. But as soon as you change you have become a different person and so your conditions must change too. This is being born again. This is the raising up of the Christ power. And if Christ be not risen, then is all our activity vain. But when the Christ power is raised up it gradually overcomes all obstacles, putting down all rule and all authority and all power of the separation belief. Finally, when the last shred of limitation belief has gone, death will be overcome too, and you will be a pillar in the temple of God and need go out no more.[12]

Adam and Eve drove themselves out of Paradise through accepting fear and doubt, but Christ reopens that eastern gate and restores them.

---

12. Revelation 3:12.

The Tower of Babel

A NYONE who has even the slightest acquaintance with the Bible knows the story of the Tower of Babel.[1] That story is so simple, so concrete, and so clear, that if you only heard it once when you were a child you could never forget it. No subtlety here. No obscure doctrines, as in some of the Epistles, just a short clear narrative, but of transcendent import.

It is, of course, a parable. The word "Babel" means confusion and, to put it briefly, this parable teaches that when you deny the omnipotence of God, and you do this whenever you give power to anything else, to matter, to climate, to fear, and so forth, only confusion and trouble can follow. To be guilty of that mistake or sin is really to have many gods, and that was the characteristic fault of the heathens. As soon as you lose the unity of God, you have lost God in your heart. Those who knew the truth about God worshiped Him and Him alone, and they received the protection and the inspiration that

_____
1. Genesis 11:1–9.

81

only the Truth can give, and as long as they were faithful to the Truth, everything went well with them. At times, however, many of those who had known the Truth, forgot it for a season, and inevitably things began to go wrong. Yet if they remembered the one God again and turned to Him wholeheartedly things would come right once more. "Thou shalt have no other gods before Me."

   If you who read this should be in difficulties of any kind it is certain that (quite unintentionally, no doubt) you have been committing the sin of the heathen in some way or perhaps several ways—you have not been putting God really first in your life, you have been giving power to some outer conditions by fearing them. It may be that at some point you have seen the higher and deliberately chosen the lower; but in any case the explanation is the same. Now if you will turn back to God once more, in your heart, and reaffirm your faith in Him, all will be well again.

The story begins by saying that *The whole earth was of one language, and of one speech.* That is to say, there was unity of thought and expression. That represents the time when your faith was firm and dynamic. Then you allowed your thought to slip away more or less from the Truth. Technically, you allowed your consciousness to fall. The second verse expresses this by saying, *And it came to pass, as they journeyed from the east, that they found a plain in the land of Shinar; and they dwelt there.*

The plain always means fear, doubt, and any kind of negative thinking in contradistinction to the hill or mountain which stands for prayer or the spiritual thought. These people allowed their thoughts to fall to a low level of selfishness and fear, and the Bible mentions the fact that this was not a momentary lapse but that they *dwelt* on that plain (or state of mind). Like the word "Babel" the word "Shinar" also means confusion. It is a very interesting fact that most names in the Bible, whether personal or geographical names, have an inner meaning that lies below the text.

The point in saying that they *dwelt* in Shinar is to stress the fact that it is not an occasional negative thought that does the harm, it is the thought or the false belief that is frequently entertained that causes your trouble.

Habitual wrong thinking, false beliefs, long entertained, not only produce fear, but they build up a conviction both conscious and subconscious that *we have to rely upon ourselves*. Of course, nothing could be more discouraging than such an idea, and in its turn it produces more fear, and so on. In that state we think less and less about God and we usually make desperate though forlorn efforts of will power.

AA

In the parable these people got the absurd idea that they could reach heaven (regain harmony) by building a material tower which would actually reach from the earth to the sky where they supposed heaven to be. Naturally, heaven is to be reached only within one's own heart by prayer and right thinking. There is no outer road to heaven, but these people were so terrorized that they were afraid of being *scattered abroad upon the face of the whole earth.*

This describes perfectly that sense of insecurity and apprehension that has always beset the greater part of mankind because they have not known or even partially realized the All-Presence and All-Power of God, and of their essential unity with Him. Jesus did not say build a material tower to the sky; he said that one should go into the secret chamber of his own heart, and close the door and realize the Presence of God.

It is easy for us to see that these people were acting in an absurd and futile way, but have we not done virtually the same thing ourselves many, many times? And, after studying this parable, we must resolve to avoid this mistake in the future as far as we possibly can.

An important point to be noted is that they decided to make their tower of brick. In the Bible, certain materials are considered noble, and certain others are considered base. Among stones, marble is the noble one and brick is the base one; and so, of course, they built their tower of brick. Brick itself, it will be noted, is an artificial product and is made of clay (of the earth earthy), whereas marble is not made by man. Also, instead of real mortar they used some kind of slime, which could hardly be expected to hold the tower together for very long. Naturally, all this is purely symbolical and it does not imply for a moment that we are not to use bricks in building our material houses or towers.

The parable also says that one of their objects in building their Babel tower was to make a *name* for themselves. In the Bible the name of anything signifies the nature of that thing, and in that sense, our "name" must come from God; for He alone can change one's nature or character for the better. *I will give him a white stone, and in the stone a new name written.*[2]

After this the account goes on to say that the Lord was angry, that He scattered the people abroad, and confounded their language so that they could not understand one another's speech. In this sense the word "Lord" means law, or rather what the people believed to be the law. It does not refer to God. Whatever we really believe is what governs our lives. We can, and we all do, make

---

2. Revelation 2:17.

laws of limitation for ourselves, and then we have to live under them. *The Lord hardened the heart of Pharaoh.*[3] This text does not mean that God hardened Pharaoh's heart for such is not the nature of God. It means that Pharaoh hardened his own heart, and told himself that he was doing the will of God. Many people throughout history have done just this, inflicting cruelty and injustice on others, and soothing their consciences by saying that it was the will of God.

The confusion of tongues is a graphic description of the state of mind of those who have not yet begun to center their lives on God, for only fear and chaos can come to them until they do.

Do not waste your time and energy in building Babel towers. They will always collapse before long and leave you worse off than ever. Babel towers are built from the ground up and with great labor; first in making the bricks themselves and then slowly piling them one on top of another. The true building or city, the new Jerusalem, is not built from the ground upward by labor, but it comes down out of heaven complete and perfect, the gift of God Himself.[4] In other words, it comes as the result of your prayers, and of your faith in the goodness of God and His unfailing providence, and the new Jerusalem brings with it harmony, peace, lasting success, and great joy.

3. Exodus 9:12.
4. Revelation 21:12.

God, the Deliverer (Psalm 18)

EVERYONE knows today that man's greatest enemy is fear. If you really get rid of fear concerning any danger it has no power to hurt you. It is no mere platitude to say, "There is nothing to fear but fear."

This wonderful Psalm is a most powerful prayer or treatment against fear. If you are afraid about something read this Psalm—or part of it—carefully and thoughtfully, realizing the spiritual meaning of each verse, and very soon your fear will begin to lessen, and will finally disappear.

The advantage of a written prayer or treatment like this is that it makes you think certain powerful healing thoughts, and, as you know, it is the right thought that demonstrates. It is not, of course, the Psalm itself but the change which it brings about in your thinking that does the work.

It opens, in the first three verses, with an affirmation of faith in God. Always begin every prayer by thinking of God, if only for a moment, and by affirming your faith and trust in Him.

86

Verse one says, *I will love thee, O Lord, my strength*. In reading this you are affirming that you are going to love God. Fear always means that one has an insufficient faith and love for God—or why should one fear?

Then you go on to say that God is your rock, and your fortress, and your *deliverer*, that God is your strength and your buckler, and that you are going to trust in Him. Then you think of Him as the horn of your salvation and your high tower. In the Bible, the horn is a symbol of power, and, of course, a high tower is a safe place and signifies a high consciousness that fear "a groundling" cannot reach, and you affirm that you will be saved from the dangers which you have been fearing.

Sometimes your fear will evaporate at this point or after a short prayer of any kind, but this is not always the case. If there is a good deal of fear it will probably take some time to overcome it. But if you hold to your faith in God it is only a question of time before you will be free and therefore safe.

At this point the Psalmist, thinking of one of his own experiences, says that the sorrows of hell compassed him about and the snares of death (great fear) prevented him, and that he "cried unto God"—he went on praying—and that God came to his rescue.

He goes on to describe how everything changed for the better as a result of his prayer, how the action of God transformed the situation from danger into perfect safety. This description is a most beautiful poem in itself. It consists of a number of graphic figures and symbols in the familiar Bible style.

He says that the earth shook and trembled and that the very hills moved because God was wroth. Of course, the "earth" means your environment, your body, and all the outer conditions that constitute your life experience at the present time. Thus the shaking and moving of these things means that all your conditions are changed, naturally for the better. The "wroth" of God in the Bible always means the *activity* of God. It does not mean anger.

1. There went up a smoke out of his nostrils, and fire out of his mouth devoured: coals were kindled by it.

2. He bowed the heavens also, and came down: and darkness was under his feet.

3. And he rode upon a cherub, and did fly: yea, he did fly upon the wings of the wind.

4. He made darkness his secret place; his pavilion round about him were dark waters and thick clouds of the skies.

5. At the brightness that was before him his thick clouds passed, hail stones and coals of fire.

6. The Lord also thundered in the heavens, and the Highest gave his voice; hail stones and coals of fire.

7. Yea, he sent out his arrows, and scattered them; and he shot out lightnings, and discomfited them.

8. Then the channels of waters were seen, and the foundations of the world were discovered at thy rebuke, O Lord, at the blast of the breath of thy nostrils.

Verse 16 sums up the experience with beautiful simplicity—*He sent from above, he took me, he drew me out of many waters.*

The writer goes on to say that God delivered him from his *strong enemy, and from them which hated me: for they were too strong for me.* Of course, the enemies, and those who hated him were his own fears and doubts, and, of course, that is true for us all.

Verse 19 says, *He brought me forth also into a large place; he delivered me, because he delighted in me.* Is it not a wonderful thought that God brings us forth into a *large* place? Does it not express dramatically the sense of being delivered from a dungeon into the open air and freedom? Then it says that he *delivered me, because he delighted in me.* God always delights in his children, and this verse really means that being delivered from the dungeon of fear, the Psalmist was beginning to experience the delight that peace of mind naturally brings.

The writer then says that God rewarded him according to his "righteousness." This word, in the Bible, always means right thinking.

And now comes a very significant statement, *according to the cleanness of my hands hath he recompensed me.* This refers to right conduct or right living. The hand always stands for activity for it represents the executive power of man. To have clean hands means that one has been trying to live the Christ life. We must never forget that our prayers have but little power if we are not honestly trying to live up to the best that we know. If we are not trying to live the life it is proof that we do not believe in our prayers, even if we think we do, for WE ALWAYS DO WHAT WE BELIEVE. It is self-deception of the deadliest kind to think "I believe such a thing although I know that I do not always do it." If you believe it, you will do it.

Next we come to one of the most profound statements of spiritual law to be found even in the Bible—*With the merciful thou wilt shew thyself merciful; with an upright man thou wilt shew thyself upright; with the pure thou wilt shew thyself pure; and with the froward thou wilt shew thyself froward.* (Verses 25 and 26)

This is a concise and powerful statement of the law that we shall literally reap what we sow. If we are merciful to others we shall receive mercy from the universe, and if we are sincere and honest, the world will be sincere and honest to us. The pure minded (and in the Bible the word "pure" means not only physical purity but loyalty to God in every phase of one's life) will be rewarded with peace and harmony that nothing can disturb. On the other hand, the froward (this word, now obsolete, means unscrupulousness of every kind) will surely bring suffering and disaster.

Naturally, the only place that you can be merciful, or upright, or pure, or froward is in your own heart, or consciousness; because that is where you rise or fall, and your words and deeds are merely the external expression of what is in your heart.

Of course, these verses do not mean literally that God sends these things. They are the automatic result of natural law. God, in His infinite wisdom, has made the laws of the universe and left them to work themselves out. He is not constantly interfering in every individual transaction as simple minded people think. If this were the case there would be no law and God would not be Principle.

To these thoughts the author adds a rider reminding us that spiritual pride leads to a fall, but that true humility and repentance always bring forgiveness. Reread the parable of the publican and the Pharisee.[1]

Now the Psalmist moves on to another phase of the teaching. He makes the reader say, or think, *Thou wilt light my candle: the Lord my God will enlighten my darkness.*

Many similes have been offered by religious teachers to illustrate the relationship between God and man. One of the best known and most helpful is to think of man as a spark from a great fire, which is God. The spark is not

---

1. Luke 18:10–14.

the whole of the fire but it is part of it, and therefore of the same nature, and possesses, potentially, all the characteristics of the parent fire. It can ignite many things upon which it falls, thus producing another fire essentially of the same nature as the original fire, and this fire grows and grows, especially if it is stimulated by a breeze. This illustrates the growth of your soul, and the breeze which builds it rapidly is, of course, prayer.

This spiritual growth will give you great power to overcome difficulties and to advance on the path. And the Psalmist, thinking of some of the times in the past when this happened to him, says, *For by thee I have run through a troop; and by my God have I leaped over a wall.* He means that he was like a single man who was able to charge through a whole troop of soldiers and they could not hold him. He also says that this help enabled him to leap over a wall. It would be a high wall, of course, or it would not be worth recording. Everyone has found himself at some time confronted with a difficulty which seemed like a high and insurmountable wall, but faith in God enables one to clear the obstacle notwithstanding.

Next he reminds us that the way of God is perfect. Prayer never brings any difficulties upon us or anyone else. It can do nothing but good. It can only improve any situation, and there is no God but the one God. When we trust to our own efforts, or, in fact, look to anything but God, "the rock," we are wasting our time. The Psalmist goes on to say once more that God will give you strength and make your way perfect. This means that your various faults and failings cannot keep you back as long as you are honestly trying to get rid of them.

It says, in the picturesque Bible way, that He will make your feet *like hinds' feet.* This implies great fleetness of foot, or quick answers to prayer.

It then says that He will put you upon your high place. In other words, He will raise your consciousness so that you will automatically demonstrate. He will teach you to pray in a still better way than you have been doing previously (teach your hands to war). He will shield you from all evil, and His right hand will hold you up. When we pray, God always acts in a gentle and kindly way and for the benefit of all concerned—*thy gentleness hath made me great.*

The next section (Verses 37 to 43), in the usual Bible idiom, graphically illustrates the demonstrations or overcomings that your prayers have brought about. Again they talk about enemies being defeated and destroyed, and, as always, these enemies are your own fears, doubts, faults, etc.

The following section deals with the dominion which you will acquire over your own mentality. The "strangers" are our most important faults and weaknesses because, familiar as they are to us in most cases, they are strangers to our real selves, and they will surely *fade away.*

Then the author praises God and thanks Him for His goodness. You probably know that thanksgiving is one of the most powerful forms of prayer.

Finally he says that God gives *great deliverance to his king;* and that *He sheweth mercy to His anointed, to David and to his seed for evermore.* You are His king. God intends us all to be kings through the exercise of spiritual power. David, in the Bible, stands for Divine Love, and the more love we have in our hearts, the more power do we have in prayer. The seed of David is our demonstrations and they are to go on increasing through all eternity.

The Zodiac and the Bible[1]

T HERE has recently been still another revival of the talk about the end of the world. Once again newspaper articles are being written and public meetings held, both in America and in Great Britain, where more or less sensational statements are made to the effect that the end of the world is now due, and may be expected at any moment. Ever since the outbreak of the Great War in 1914 the prophets have been exceptionally busy in this direction, and on several occasions groups of people have actually sat up all night waiting for the end.

Now the old adage says that there is no smoke without fire, and it proves itself in the present instance, for behind all this speculation and discussion a great truth

1. Being the Substance of a Lecture delivered by Emmet Fox at Victoria Hall, London, on September 6, 1933. Readers will note that the present reprint was first published in the spring of 1938, nearly five years afterward, and that some of the world changes predicted have already taken place.

93

undoubtedly does lie, and in this chapter I propose to explain exactly what it is.

The actual fact is that, while it is not true that the end of the world in the ordinary sense of the words is coming upon us, we do indeed stand on the threshold of a new age. One age has now passed away and another age is coming into being, and it is this tremendous change in the unfoldment of the human race that people of all sorts everywhere have been sensing. In other words, humanity is now entering upon a new era in its history, and this means that most of the old ideas in which we were all brought up are now definitely become out of date, and that we shall have to adapt ourselves to a completely new outlook upon life. A completely new outlook, mark you—no mere rearrangement of old ideas into a new pattern, such as the changing of a monarchy into a republic or a republic into a monarchy, the disestablishing of one church and the establishing of a rival one, the swapping of King Log for King Stork, or the changing of Tweedledum for Tweedledee. It means a complete change in all our fundamental values, a completely new way of looking at all human problems—in fact a new age.

Many people are looking about them today with a feeling of consternation at what they see in the world. Old landmarks, like the Austrian Empire, the Czarist Empire, the Hohenzollern Empire, and the Turkish Empire, are swept away within four short years. The ancient Chinese Empire in the East and the Spanish Monarchy in the West have disappeared too. The greatest material boom in recorded history has been followed by the greatest depression. The Governor of the Bank of England has publicly stated that after months of investigation he does not understand the causes of the depression, and that he has

no remedy to offer for dealing with it. The orthodox
churches were once hardly adequate to meet the needs
of a smaller population, and now churchmen complain
of the empty pews that face them Sunday after Sunday;
and the reason is that the old theological sanctions which
once meant so much are no longer taken seriously by
the great masses of the people. In fact, it is often said bitterly that nothing is as it was; everything is changed. General Smuts said a year or two ago, "Humanity has once
more struck its tents, and is again on the march."

All this is perfectly correct, as far as it goes, but when
once we have the key to the mainspring of human history we shall no longer be either surprised or dismayed
at these occurrences. No matter what the next few years
may hold—and beyond a doubt they are going to show
us some very surprising things—we shall not be either
alarmed or grieved if we realize what it is that is really
happening.

The history of mankind proceeds in no haphazard or
casual way, but through the unfoldment of a number of
distinct periods or ages. Each of these periods has its own
characteristics, its own lessons to be learned, its own work
to be done; and each one is quite fundamentally different in every respect from its predecessor and not a mere
improvement or expansion of it. Each of these ages lasts
approximately two thousand years; to be more precise,
each one is usually about two thousand, one hundred
and fifty years long; and the passing from one such age
into another is always accompanied by both external and
internal storm and stress such as the world has recently
been going through. The last change took place a couple
of thousand years ago, and the new world that formed
itself from that melting pot was the western Christian civilization that we know. This great enterprise having

worked itself out and fulfilled its mission, has now drawn to its close, and the new age is already upon us.

In connection with the coming and going of these different ages it is necessary to be familiar with the natural phenomenon known as the Precession of the Equinoxes. It is not necessary that a student should possess any general knowledge of astronomy; it is sufficient to know that as we look out from our globe at the illimitable starry hosts that surround us, the axis of the earth seems to trace out a huge circle in the heavens every twenty-six thousand years or thereabouts. This huge circle, which is known as the Zodiac, falls into twelve parts or sectors, and each part, or "Sign," as the Ancients called it, marks the passage of time that we occupy in working through one of our "Ages."

This "Zodiac" is one of the most interesting of all the symbols that reveal the destiny of mankind. In fact, the Zodiac with its twelve signs, symbolizes the most fundamental thing in the nature of man. It is nothing less than the key to the history of the Human Race, of the psychology of the individual man, and of his regeneration or spiritual salvation. The Bible, which is of course the great fountain of Truth, has the Zodiac running through it from beginning to end. The twelve sons of Jacob who become the twelve tribes of the Old Testament, and the twelve Apostles of the New Testament, are, apart from their historical identity, special expressions of the twelve signs of the Zodiac. The marshalling of the Twelve Tribes of Israel in strict astronomical order in the great encampment of the wilderness is a leading example of this Zodiacal symbolism which the reader can check for himself.

The knowledge of this mysterious thing, the Zodiac, is found all over the world, among all races, and in all ages. Excavations among the most ancient ruins in Asia have revealed representations of the Zodiac. Both the earlier and the later Egyptians understood it well. The Chaldeans were masters of the subject. It was engraved upon the temples of Greece and Rome. The American aborigines in Mexico and Peru were well acquainted with it; the oldest Chinese records speak of it; and it has turned up unexpectedly on forgotten islands in the Pacific. Pythagoras taught it in the olden days, of course; and it was incorporated into the fabric of more than one of the medieval cathedrals. The Great Circle at Stonehenge is really a type of the Zodiac; and the twelve Signs, beautifully executed, form part of the ornamentation of several of the very newest and highest skyscrapers in New York.

Now what is the real significance of the Zodiac which so universally permeates all human culture? It is a curious and most interesting fact that men constantly employ, and thus perpetuate, symbols of whose real meaning they are not consciously aware. Often in this way the profoundest truths are enshrined in what seems to be but a casual ornamentation.

The Zodiac has usually been either ignored, or treated as a mere picturesque decoration, or else it has been degraded into superstition and fortune telling; and so we have now to ask ourselves the question—What is the real significance of the Zodiac? And in order to answer that question we must put another one—What is the real reason of mankind being on the earth at all? What are we here for? What is it all about? Why are we born, and why do we die? Is there a reason or a pattern behind it all? And if so, what is it? And the answer to these questions, no doubt the most fundamental of all questions, is this: That we are here to learn the Truth of Being. That we are here to become self-conscious, self-governed entities, focal points of the Divine Mind, each expressing God in a new way. That is the object of our existence, and the only thing that we have to do to realize it is to get a better knowledge of God, because such knowledge is the answer to every problem. All trouble, all sin, sickness, poverty, accidents, death itself, are due simply to a want of knowledge of God, and, per contra, all health, success, prosperity, beauty, joy and happiness consist in obtaining that knowledge of God. When we are in trouble of any kind it means that for the time being our knowledge of God is inadequate; and recovery means that our knowledge of God has become clearer.

Of course, some individuals progress far more rapidly than the main bulk. These are the leaders and teachers of the race. But the main body of humanity is always steadily, if it may seem a little slowly, growing in its knowledge of God. This is the reality behind what we call progress, or evolution. The passage from savagery to barbarism, and from barbarism on to civilization is really a growth in the knowledge of God. All the things that we see as scientific, artistic, or social advancement; such diverse things as the spread of hygiene, universal and compulsory education, the abolition of slavery, and the emancipation of women; all these things are really but the outer expression of mankind's increase in the true knowledge of God.

In order to acquire that full understanding of all that God is, that full understanding which will be his complete salvation, man has to learn, piecemeal as it were, to know God in twelve different ways. It takes him a couple of thousand years to learn each of these lessons; and so, we can, if we like, think of our progress around the Zodiac as a series of twelve lessons that we have to learn about God. We have now finished our last lesson, and have already begun our study of the new one.

Each of these lessons has a name which has been allotted to it for convenience. Everything must have a name, but, as many of us know, names when rightly understood are often found to be symbolical of the things for which they stand, and the names of our lessons or "Signs" are no exception to this rule. The name of the last sign, the one which we have just left, was Pisces, or the Fishes. The one before that, which we left over two thousand years ago, was Aries, or the Ram. The one before that was Taurus, or the Bull, and so forth. These names, be it noted, do not in the least refer to the physical shape of the constellations as seen in the sky—much effort has been wasted in the endeavor to trace a far-fetched resemblance to a lion, or a bull, or a centaur, where there is not the very faintest ground for so doing—they refer to the innate character of the lesson that we have to learn at the particular time that is indicated by the Sign.

The new age upon which we have now entered is called Aquarius—the Man with the Water Pot—and the Aquarian Age is going to be a completely new chapter in the history of mankind. The student should be very clear about this. A new age means everything new, and not just a polishing up of the old Piscean ideas which most people make the mistake of regarding as the only possible ideas—the only natural and established order of things—instead of being merely one of an infinite number of possible expressions.

As a matter of fact, we are, within the not very far distant future, going to change everything in the outer world around us. Our political, social, and ecclesiastical institutions, our methods of doing our daily work, our relationships with one another, our manifold instruments of self-expression and self-discovery—all will undergo a change, a radical change, and for the better. A few of these changes have already come about, but the really big changes are yet to be.

Now, concerning these changes, it will be the attitude which the individual adopts toward them which will determine their reaction upon him. If we take up an attitude of resistance to these natural changes, if we, so to say, antagonize them in our own consciousness, if we assume that change must necessarily be bad—which is only another way of saying that all our present arrangements are perfect and unimprovable—then we shall suffer a sense of conflict, and defeat, and loss. We shall go about saying, "the country is going to the dogs"; talk foolishly about "the good old days" (which never existed); and, in fact, take up the stock attitude of obscurantism and reaction. Our soul will become, what was said of a certain university, "a home of lost causes and dead faiths." And all this will mean, temporarily at least, defeat, failure, and waste.

If, on the other hand, we know the Truth and practice it, we shall sweep forward in the grand march of humanity, learning the new lesson, rejoicing in the new work, and triumphing in its triumphs. If, instead of seeking to hold on to the wreckage of outworn things, we are prepared to march breast forward and, as has been finely said, "greet the unknown with a cheer," then indeed shall we be loyal servants of God and of our fellow men. The summing up of all wisdom is also the fundamental recipe for happiness, "Set your heart upon God, and not upon things, upon Cause and not upon manifestation, upon Principle and not upon form." As the old landmarks disappear one by one beneath the rising tide of the new life, we shall go boldly on, knowing that the best is yet to be, and that "Eye hath not seen, nor ear heard, neither hath it entered into the heart of man the things that God hath prepared for them that love Him," and put Him first.

Each of these Ages or ways of knowing God has a dominant quality or character of its own which distinguishes it from the other eleven. Just as each nation has an indefinable quality which all its natives possess in common, no matter how much they may otherwise differ among themselves, and which marks them off from all other groups of people; just as each of the great religions has its own special character or atmosphere that arises from the particular aspects of Universal Truth upon which it lays stress, so each Age has its own peculiar character arising from the particular aspects of Truth with which it deals. The quality which distinguishes the new Aquarian Age—so distinct in every respect from the late Piscean Age—is called for convenience "Uranus," and in a general way all the activities and expressions of the Aquarian Age will be Uranian. Now this is interesting because it gives us a broad idea of the sort of thing that we may expect. Uranus is usually spoken of as a disrupter or smasher, but it must be remembered that this does not necessarily, as is too often assumed, imply real destruction. It is well that the less good should be destroyed if this means that the better is given an opportunity of taking its place. Those who understand the Truth of Being are well aware that what we call death and destruction are usually but the prelude to something better and finer. What is the death of Monday but the birth of Tuesday, the death of the old year but the birth of the new one, the pulling down of an old house but the prelude to the building of a newer and better one. And so the New Age, while at first it may seem to be destructive, will, in fact, be destructive only of ideas which, while good and necessary in their own time, have now been outgrown by humanity, and could only remain as a hindrance.

Consider the state of mind of the chick at the moment when he has become fully formed and ready for a free and independent life; but just before the shell has broken. How delightfully comfortable the inside of that shell feels. How warm, how snug, how safe. How terrifying to a nervous chick must be the prospect of being thrown out into a wide, cold, unknown, seemingly infinite world. Yet, because he is now mature and ready for the great adventure, the warm shell which has been so necessary and so comforting to him up to that moment, would, if he attempted to remain in it, very soon smother and destroy him. He has outgrown that phase, and out he must go, willing or not. A brave chick, on the contrary, one who has faith in the essential goodness of life, and the innate friendliness of things, goes out into the new world conquering and to conquer. Here Uranus comes, as a smasher indeed but it is as the smasher of a prison, and the liberator of a captive soul.

Humanity is now very much in the position of the chick who has outgrown his old environment, and must boldly step out into something new and strange and grand.

Uranus is also spoken of as a symbol of democracy and freedom, and at other times it is referred to as standing for autocracy; and this seeming contradiction has puzzled many; but the actual truth is that Uranus stands neither for democracy nor autocracy as such, but for *individuality*. Now the free expression of individuality must mean true democracy in the sense that every human soul shall have an equal opportunity for self-expression as the thing that God intended it to be, and, on the other hand, as the master of its own fate and the captain of its own soul, it becomes the autocrat of its own life, answerable to God alone and unrestricted in its development by any tyrannical outside interference. That is Uranus.

We have actually been in the Aquarian Age for a number of years already, but it is only now that we are beginning to feel the full effects of the change. Nature knows nothing of sudden jerky transitions. With her all is gradual, and so each New Age steals slowly upon the human consciousness, and more than one generation goes by before the changes become easily observable. We must remember that in a period lasting about twenty-one hundred and fifty years, half a century or a century does not mean so much as one might suppose at first sight. Today the introductory period technically known as the "cusp" is over, and we are now in the full tide of Aquarian life. As we look about us in the world we are at once struck by the number of Aquarian manifestations everywhere in being. The new inventions, for instance, that have transformed the world since the childhood of middle-aged people, are nearly all Aquarian-Uranian in character. Electricity, which in its various forms, as electric light and traction, the telegraph and the telephone, and now the radio, has done so much to make the new world different from the old one—electricity is essentially Uranian. Every application of electricity, for instance, is the individualization at a particular point of manifestation— lamp, motor, bell, microphone, and so forth—of a general current. And everyone who has experimented however slightly, with an electric current knows that when wrongly handled it is exceedingly sudden and violent in its reactions—a disrupter or wrecker. Yet, when employed constructively and intelligently, it does more than any other material thing to liberate the human soul from the fetters of drudgery and physical limitations. The telephone abolishes distance and is man's first partial demonstration over the space limitation. The electric light indoors and out-of-doors has been the finger of God in promoting education, cleanliness, sanitation, and all other good things that wither in darkness and flourish in light. Electric traction, when it is given a fair chance, will empty our city slums and restore our people to God's countryside. The radio is rapidly breaking down many of the artificial barriers that formerly divided man from man. Within each nation it is destroying social prejudices right and left by giving a correct standard of speech to all classes, and already the change wrought by this is quite noticeable. Internationally the radio laughs at frontiers, and, thanks to its efforts, it will no longer be possible, however much reactionary authorities may desire it, to isolate any body of human beings from the common stock of human knowledge and human progress. The Inquisition would have been powerless against the radio broadcast and a receiving set in every home.

Next to electricity the internal combustion engine in the form of the automobile and the airplane has probably done most to change the face of the world, and this too is essentially Uranian-Aquarian. Consider how fundamentally individual a thing an automobile is, as compared say with the railroad train. Indeed, one could hardly get a more complete expression of the distinction between mass compulsion and free individuality than in considering the difference between taking a prescribed journey to a prescribed time-table in a train and the untrammeled exploring of the countryside in a car. Internationally the airplane has simply abolished military frontiers. Military authors are still writing in terms of strategic frontiers, but statesmen know to their secret consternation that they are gone.

The Aquarian Age, in fact, is to be the age of personal freedom. It is no mere coincidence that its arrival marks the emancipation of women as a sex, and that in the present age the children too have at last been conceded rights as individuals, and are no longer regarded simply as the personal property of their parents.

We have seen that what are called the Twelve Signs of the Zodiac really signify twelve different ways of knowing God. Most thinking people have already given up the old childish way of thinking of God as just a big superior kind of man, and as the Aquarian Age advances the great bulk of mankind will gradually outgrow that limitation too. The truth is that actually God is All in All: Infinite Mind, Life, Truth, and Love. God is Infinite Intelligence, Unfathomable Wisdom, Unspeakable Beauty. In repeating these words, we get, of course, a hopelessly inadequate realization of what they must really mean, and the true nature of God in its fullness is so immense and wonderful and undreamed of by us, that in practice it takes the human race not thousands, but millions of years to reach its full comprehension. Even to grasp the fact that God is Incorporeal Mind, perfect Principle, has taken us literally hundreds of thousands of years; and we shall not all reach even this point for some time to come yet. And when we have grasped that stupendous reality, the Truth about God still opens out in front of us to Infinity.

Just as each Age is a special lesson that humanity has to learn about God, so in each Age there is a special outstanding teacher who teaches the lesson of that Age, and demonstrates it in a complete and unmistakable manner. The great Race Teacher of the Age of Aries was

Abraham. Abraham raised the standard of the One God, perfect, not made with hands, eternal in the heavens. Abraham when he received his enlightenment came straight out from idolatry and, forestalling Moses, said, in effect—Know, O Israel the Lord thy God is One God— Thou shalt have no other gods before Him—Thou shalt not make unto thyself graven images.

How tremendous a step forward this was in the history of humanity, can only be appreciated by those who have investigated the old civilizations, with their welter of competing gods, and their futile, grotesque, and sometimes obscene idolatries. An old tradition tells that the immediate family of Abram (as he then was) were actually manufacturers and sellers of idols, and so, in coming out for the One purely Spiritual God, he was obliged to break with his own immediate people. It may well have been so, for is it not the maker of images who is most likely, given an honest heart, to become the iconoclast.

Abraham, having launched the new Age, that of Aries or the Ram, passed into history, and his work went on with the usual ebb and flow characteristic of human activity. Now it should be noted that that Age is called symbolically the Age of the Ram or Sheep, and that all through the Bible sheep are used to symbolize thoughts, and that the great outstanding lesson of the Bible is that we have to watch our thoughts, because whatever we think with conviction will come to us sooner or later. It is important to note in this connection how many of the great saints and heroes of the Bible were at one time shepherds. Jacob, Moses, David, Cyrus the Mede ("His Anointed"), and many of lesser importance all served an apprenticeship in the keeping of sheep—the right control of thought. And of the many titles that have been given to our Lord himself, he would probably have preferred that of the Good

Shepherd. Did he not say, "The Good Shepherd gives his life for his sheep." In all this we see the influence of the Ariean lesson working itself out in the race thought. Egypt, in the Bible, stands for materialism, sin, sickness, and death ("Out of Egypt have I called my son") and very significantly we are told that the Egyptians harbored an undying enmity and hatred for a shepherd. All this, of course, is not to be taken literally as a reflection upon the people who lived in the Nile valley, and were no worse, if no better, than other men, but as a symbolical description of the working out of natural laws. It is an interesting fact that right down to the present day in the Jewish synagogues where the Ariean Age still lingers, the Ram's horn remains as a living symbol.

The Age which followed the Ariean Age, and from which we have recently emerged, and which might well be called the epoch of orthodox Christianity, is known as the Age of Pisces or the Fishes. The great leader and prophet of that Age was, of course, Jesus Christ, and we know that in the early days of Christianity he was symbolized among his followers as a fish. The cross, the great emblem of Christianity in later times, was not used in the first days. People were then a little ashamed to think of the Master in connection with a Roman gibbet. In the catacombs of Rome and elsewhere we find inscriptions of the early Christians in which Jesus is referred to as the fish. This had the further advantage of throwing their persecutors off the scent. Actually, the cross as a symbol of physical matter and physical limitation, is far, far older than Christianity; but that is by the way. Suffice it to say that the Age of Pisces was constantly being announced in symbols by all sorts of people, many of whom realized not at all what it was that they were doing. The great medieval church, for instance, centered her authority, for practical purposes, in the bishop, and the distinguishing symbol of a bishop is, of course, the mitre. And what is the mitre but a fish's head worn as a headdress. Jesus said, "I will make you fishers of men," and actually his first disciples were fishermen, just as the Old Testament leaders were shepherds.

All through the Bible, and throughout the old occult tradition in general, the fish stands as a symbol of wisdom, and wisdom is then understood as the technical term for the knowledge of the Allness of God and of the power of prayer. Notice that the fish lives in the depths of the waters (the human soul) from which it has to be, so to say, fished out, and it is silent and non-assertive. It has to be sought with patience and gentleness. It is not to be hunted down violently as is a wolf.

The Aquarian Age is the age of the Man with the Water Pot ("Seek ye a man bearing a pot of water")—and who is the man with the water pot? Why, the gardener, of course, and so the interpretative symbol of the New Age is to be the Gardener. Man having graduated as a Shepherd, and as a Fisherman, now becomes a Gardener, and this title nicely expresses the kind of work that he has to do in his new rôle. We have now reached the stage when the lesson of the need for thought control having been learned, and the *Santa Sophia* or Holy Wisdom having been contacted and appreciated, the two things must be united mentally in our everyday practice.

Modern science is making some of its greatest strides in the realm of psychology, so that indeed psychology may today be called the handmaid of metaphysics, and psychology is insisting more and more that the conscious and the subconscious minds stand almost exactly in the relationship of gardener and garden. The gardener sows his seed in the soil that he has prepared; he waters the ground and, as far as possible, he selects a site upon which the sun will shine; but he does not try to make the seed grow. He leaves that to Nature. So, in spiritual treatment or Scientific Prayer, we speak the Word, but we leave it to the Divine Power to make the demonstration. "I have planted; Apollos watered; but God gave the increase." The dominant note of the New Age is to be Spiritual development and Spiritual demonstration.

At this stage the question naturally presents itself— Who is, or who is to be, the great teacher and prophet of our new Aquarian Age? Well, it seems that there is no lack of candidates for the position. All over the world sundry people are laying claim to this high office, or their followers are claiming it for them. No time need be wasted over this sort of thing. Did not the Master warn us that false Christs would arise who would deceive, if it were possible, the very elect.

The wonderful fact is that now, after all these thousands and thousands of years of upward striving, we have at last reached the stage where humanity is ready to do without personal prophets of any kind, and to contact the Living God at first hand for itself. Never until now has this been possible for the mass of the people. Individuals from time to time have reached this stage, but never until now has it been possible for the great majority. Always they have had to have some concrete symbol. First of all, a coarse and palpable idol such as was denounced by Abraham and Moses, and afterward by Mohammed. Later when they had passed beyond that stage, they still demanded a man to worship, or even a book, something tangible and concrete to lay hold of mentally. But now, chiefly owing to the work that Jesus did in the race mind nineteen hundred years ago, it has become possible for all men and women, if they will, to grasp the idea of the Impersonal Christ Truth; <u>to grasp the truth that their own Indwelling Christ—the Inner Light of the Quakers—is always with them to inspire, to heal, to strengthen and comfort, and illumine.</u> Jesus said, unless I go away the Holy Spirit cannot come, meaning that as long as he was with them they would cling to his personality instead of finding the Infinite, Incorporeal God for themselves; and this is very largely what the orthodox churches have always done.

<u>And so the Great World Teacher of the new age is not to be any man or woman, or any textbook, or any organization, but the Indwelling Christ, that each individual is to find and contact for himself.</u> There is a simple test by which anyone can tell a true teacher from a false one. It is this: If he points you to his own personality; if he makes special claims for himself; if he says that he has received any special privileges from God that are not equally accessible to the whole human race anywhere; if he attempts in his own name or in that of an organization to establish under any pretense a monopoly of the truth about God, then, however imposing his credentials, however pleasing his personality may be, he is a false teacher, and you had better have nothing to do with him. If, on the contrary, he tells you to look away from himself, to seek the Presence of God in your own heart, and to use books, lectures, and churches only as a means to that one end, then, however humble his efforts may be, however lacking his own demonstration may seem, he is nevertheless a true teacher and is giving you the Bread of Life.

It takes humanity about twenty-six thousand years to go through this class of twelve lessons about God, which we call the Zodiac. <u>But of course, we have been through that class many times already—remember that the race is far older than most people think—and we shall have to</u>

go through it many times more, but each time we go through the same lessons at a much higher level, garnering a different *quality* of knowledge, for it is not an endless circle, but an upward reaching spiral.

Now this change through which the world is going at the present time, which is covering the front pages of the newspapers with sensations, and filling the hearts of men with fear and misgivings, this change, as it happens, is much more than the mere passing from one Sign or Age to another, such as happened in passing from Aries into Pisces, from Taurus into Aries, from Gemini into Taurus, and so on. Actually our present change is the greatest that the human race has made for about fifty-two thousand years. That is to say, we have been twice around the Zodiac since we last made such a giant step forward as the present one. Not since the mass of humanity became capable of using the abstract mind (it is quite true that precious few of them ever use it now, but they all could if they wanted to and were trained for it) has it gained such an increase in Power. It is now possible for everyone if he so wishes to contact the Spiritual Power which lies all around us, which is God, always ready at a moment's notice to help us in any way we may need.

This means that while the race as a whole moves forward relatively slowly on the path of spiritual development, *there is now no reason at all why any individual who really desires it should not cut out all intermediate steps and make the Great Demonstration at his own pace, irrespective of any material circumstances of time, or Zodiac, or anything else whatever.* The qualities he will need for success are a single-minded pursuit of Truth and the wholehearted practice of the highest that he knows at the moment.

So now we see that the Zodiac is really one of the great cosmic symbols, perhaps the greatest of them all, a diagram of the unfoldment of the human soul, and not the mere physical fact of the Precession of the Equinoxes. Not just a kind of circular railroad track for fortune-telling, but one of the deepest mysteries of the soul.

The question of *when* the great changes herein referred to will take place is naturally one that does not admit of a precise answer. It may, however, be said with confidence that what will appear to us as the most revolutionary and far-reaching upheavals in the circumstances of human life will be all over and done with in from twenty to twenty-five years from now; and that some very striking and important changes are already under way and will become perhaps startlingly apparent within the next few years.

These changes will hardly go through without a certain amount of disturbance and temporary chaos, as we have seen; but we know that Man as a race will emerge with flying colors, purified, strengthened, and emancipated. But what of the individual? Well, individuals may have a bad time in certain cases, but your personal fate will depend upon one thing, and one thing only—the condition in which you keep your consciousness. If you maintain an attitude of mental peace and goodwill toward all; if you really root out of your own heart every atom of hostility and condemnation for your brother man, no matter who he may be, then you will be safe. As Jesus promised: "Nothing shall by any means hurt you." You will pass through the hottest fires unmoved and unscathed. But, if you allow yourself to be drawn, if only by mental acquiescence, into any current of hatred against anybody, against any nation, or any race, or any class or any religious sect, or any other person or body of people, under any pretense whatsoever; then you will have forfeited your protection and you will have to take the consequences. If you allow yourself to be carried away by any political, religious, or newspaper campaign of hatred, no matter how self-righteously it may be camouflaging itself, then you will be laying yourself open to any destructive tendencies that may be going. It is for you to choose, knowing that as you do choose, so it will be done unto you.

Of course, the only real protection in any kind of danger is the knowledge of Scientific Prayer, or the Practice of the Presence of God; and so have not we who understand this Truth and how to apply it in practice, a sacred duty and responsibility to do all that lies in our power to spread that knowledge now as widely and as quickly as possible.

The Seven Main Aspects of God

H AVE you ever asked yourself the question: What is God like? We are told to pray by turning away from the problem and thinking about God; but how are we to think about God? What is His nature? What is His character? Where is He? Can we really contact Him, and if so, how?

The first and most fundamental thing to realize is that God is not just a superior kind of man. Most people would say, "Of course not"; but my experience shows me that even today the majority of people, in their hearts, do think of God as just a magnified man—that and nothing more—a very good man, an extraordinarily wise man, a man of infinite power, but still a man. Now such an idea is really but a projection of their own personalities, and it requires very little thought to show that such an idea cannot be true. In philosophy, such a being is called an anthropomorphic God (from anthropos—man, and morphe—form—see *Webster's*). And no such finite person could possibly have created the boundless universe that we see through our telescopes, or the infinite variety of

114

minute forms that we contact through the microscope; to say nothing of the infinite creation of which we are still altogether unaware.

It is natural for a thoughtless person to think of God as being just a bigger edition of himself, just as we may suppose that if an insect could think of God, he would think of Him as an enormous insect of unlimited power. We, however, are beings possessing the twin faculties of reason and intuition, and so we must get beyond this infantile stage to the truth.

God is infinite which is in-finite or unlimited. Reflect upon this every day of your life and a lifetime will not be long enough to grasp all that it means. For instance, you could not go into a room or a building to meet God because if God could be located in a particular room He would not be infinite. What usually happens is that while we are still very young, small children, we form ideas (childish ones naturally) about all sorts of things. We think a three-story house is a skyscraper. We think the road near which we live is so wide that crossing it is quite a journey. We think our parents know everything and could do anything. At that stage we think of God as being like our grandfather, or perhaps like the clergyman at the local church. Then we begin to grow up, and, as maturity comes, we gradually revise our ideas upon all subjects except one. We revise our ideas about our family, our city, and our country; about business, and sport, and politics; but in most cases people never revise their early idea of God; and so they continue in years of maturity to try to get along with the idea of God that they formed in infancy, and naturally the result is very limiting. It is really as though the grown man tried to wear the shoes of the infant. He could not walk at all.

A great practical difficulty in discussing God is the fact that we have no suitable pronoun to employ. We have to use the words "he" and "him." We have no alternative, but these words are very misleading because they inevitably suggest a man or male animal. To say "she" and "her" would be equally absurd, and the word "it," besides seeming to lack in reverence, suggests an inanimate and unintelligent object. The reader is therefore asked to bear in mind that the use of "He" and "Him" is an unavoidable makeshift, and to correct his thought accordingly.

The Bible says that God is spirit[1] and that they that worship Him must worship Him in spirit and in truth. To worship Him in spirit means to get a spiritual understanding of His nature, and we shall now endeavor to do this. We shall not attempt to define God because that would be to limit Him, but we can get what is for all practical purposes an excellent working knowledge of God. We shall do this by considering different aspects of His nature, one by one.

Suppose you wanted to see a great building like the Capitol in Washington. You know that you cannot possibly see it all at once, but that does not mean that you cannot become very well acquainted with it. What you must do is to walk around the building, viewing it from different angles until you have seen it all. You would look at it, let us say, from the north, and then from the east, and then from the south, and then from the west; and then you would know exactly what the building looked like. We shall do the same with the idea of God.

The only way to approach God is by thinking of Him. There are no material steps that will bring you to God.

---

1. John 4:24, Revised Version.

Only by thinking of Him can you approach Him. In the East, certain foolish people have tried to get close to God by maiming their bodies or by assuming unnatural and uncomfortable postures, or training themselves to difficult feats of acrobatics—but such things are a waste of time. There is no way to find God except by *prayer*, and prayer is thinking about God.

There are three degrees of intensity in prayer. The first and easiest way is to pray aloud, what is often called an audible treatment. The second degree, which is a little more difficult for most people but is also much more powerful, is to think systematically about God, recognizing His presence where the trouble seems to be. This is meditation, and a good way to meditate is to read a verse of the Bible, or a paragraph from a spiritual book and then let your mind work on it. The third degree is reached when the thought and thinker become one and there is a vivid realization of Truth. This is called contemplation, but it is not possible for most people to attain to it yet, and one should never try to do so. At the right time it will come spontaneously, and before the right time you cannot compel it. Most practical problems can be solved by sufficient audible prayer or meditation.

God is infinite, but we, as human beings, while we cannot of course grasp the Infinite, can yet acquaint ourselves with many different aspects or attributes of His nature. Of these there are Seven Main Aspects that are more important than any of the others. These are seven fundamental truths about God, and all the others are built up of combinations of some of these seven. These truths never change. They were the same a billion years ago and they will be the same a billion years hence. So naturally it behooves us to get as clear an understanding and as strong a realization as possible of these Seven

Main Aspects. This can be done by thinking about them a good deal, comparing one with another, and identifying them in the experiences of everyday life. This is prayer, and very powerful prayer too. The quickest way to solve a particular problem is to meditate on whichever aspect is the most appropriate in that particular case. Thinking of *any* Aspect of God will solve a problem, but if you select the right Aspect you will get your result more quickly and more easily.

The FIRST MAIN ASPECT I am going to consider is Life. God is Life. God is not just living, nor does God *give* life, but God *is* Life. Where God is, there Life is. God is your life. Life is existence or being.

When you are sick you are only partly alive. When you are tired or depressed or discouraged, you are only partly alive. To be truly alive means to be well and full of interest in the day's work. Few people as yet express God in an adequate way because they lack the sense of life. What usually happens is that people grow up to a maximum sense of life, what we call the "prime" of life, and then gradually deterioration sets in, a process which we call "middle age," and finally come old age and death. This process is common to the whole race, and is not, of course, the fault of the individual. But we have to overcome it some time by realizing that it is only a false belief, and by knowing (not merely believing) that God is our Life and that He never changes.

Joy is one of the highest expressions of God as Life. Actually it is a mixture of Life and Love, and the Bible says that "the sons of God shout for joy." This means that when we realize our divine sonship, we must experience joy, and that sorrow is a loss of the sense of the fatherhood of God. Joy and happiness always have an expansive effect, just as fear has a contracting and paralyzing effect. You know how a little child, when it meets someone whom it loves and trusts, expands like an opening flower and goes out to meet him, but when it is afraid, shrinks back into itself. That is what happens to the human soul too. Again, when a person says "I can," you always notice an expansive and forward movement, but when he says "I can't," there is a retraction. You could not imagine a person saying "Yes, I can," with a shrinking gesture, or "No, I can't," in an optimistic or forthright way. The body always expresses the thought; and the thought of Life heals and inspires, whereas thoughts of fear and death contract and destroy.

You should realize the Aspect of God as Life for healing sickness, for the "getting older" belief, and for any kind of depression or discouragement.

Realizing Divine Life heals a sick person, and, of course, you can heal animals and plants too. Animals usually respond quickly to this treatment, and plants very quickly indeed; but one should not try to keep an old animal alive by treatment after it has reached the normal span for its species. Animals and plants yield quickly because they do not have that strong sense of personal egotism that most human beings do. They never make up their minds that they cannot get well or that "sickness is sent for a good purpose." Neither do they give way to discouragement because they have not been healed faster.

An excellent experiment is to select two plants or two flower beds and start them off together. Then treat one of them every day, but not the other, and before long you will be surprised to find how much difference there is in the progress made by them. Realize the presence of Divine Life in the flower bed or plant and give it thoughts of Love—drench it with Love. Everyone knows that some gardeners are far more successful than others, even though their technical qualifications may be the same, and the reason is that one loves his plants and the other has only a business interest in them.

If a person seems to lack ambition treat him for life by realizing the presence of Divine Life in him. A man came to me whose grown-up son seemed to be quite without ambition. On my advice the father treated him by realizing Divine Life, and very soon things began to change. The patient lost his listlessness, began to take an interest in life, and was soon doing well at his work. The doctors told the father that the patient's glands were working better, and no doubt the treatment did improve them, but, of course, this was only the channel or means by which the prayer acted.

Here is another interesting experiment that you can make. Some evening when you find yourself in a crowded streetcar or subway train, and most of the people around you are looking tired and worried and obviously wishing they were at their journey's end, just start declaring the Presence of God as Life in all those present; and keep it up. You will be surprised and gratified at what will happen. First one person will brighten up and smile, and then another will obviously relax, and before long the whole crowd in that car will be feeling and looking differently. Do not say that this is fantastic nonsense, but try it.

The SECOND MAIN ASPECT of God is Truth. God is Truth. God is not truthful but Truth itself, and wherever there is Truth, there is God. God is absolute Truth and does not change. There are many things which are relatively true at certain times and places only; but God is absolute Truth at all times and in all circumstances. As soon as we touch God who is the Absolute, relative things disappear.

To know the Truth about any condition heals it. Jesus said, "Know the truth, and the truth shall make you free."[2] Truth is the great healer.

You should realize God as Truth when you want information on any subject, or if you suspect that you have to deal with deceit or falsehood. If you have reason to believe that someone is trying to deceive you, think of God as Truth and claim that Divine Truth dwells in the person concerned, and is expressed through him. If you realize this clearly enough he will then speak the truth. When you have to transact any important business such as signing a lease or a contract, spend a few minutes realizing Divine Truth and if there is anything you should know it will come out. Of course, people may have no desire to deceive you and yet for some reason you may not be given the whole story. I know of several cases where serious misunderstandings were prevented because somebody realized God as Truth and so all the facts were brought out. I know also of several cases where intentional dishonesty was frustrated in the same way.

Realizing God as Truth will save you hours of work in research in any field. You will be led to the right book or the right place or the right person without loss of time, or the necessary information will come to you in some other way.

The THIRD MAIN ASPECT of God is Love. God is Love. God is not loving but Love itself, and it would probably be true to say that of all the Seven Main Aspects this is the most important one for us in practice. There is no

---

2. John 8:32.

condition that enough Love will not heal,[3] and where there is good will it is not difficult to develop a sufficient sense of Love for the purpose of healing. The whole Bible deals with the nature of God, and as the Scripture develops, the idea of God becomes clearer and clearer until toward the end it says, "God is love; and he that dwelleth in love dwelleth in God, and God in him,"[4] and higher than this we cannot go. Jesus himself said, "By this shall all men know that ye are my disciples, if ye have love one to another."[5]

Where there is fear there cannot be love. The best way to rid yourself of fear is to realize Divine Love. When you love God more than you love your problem, you will be healed. Does that seem strange to you? It is true. If you love God more than you love your microbe, your sickness, your grievance, your lack, or your fear, you will be healed. If you could feel a sense of Divine Impersonal Love toward everyone, no one could hurt you. If someone came to rob you or kill you he would not be able to carry out his intention. We have all heard many stories of exceptional people who were able to go among wild beasts in the jungle without being hurt, and there are many other histories on record of people who passed through extraordinary dangers of other kinds quite unscathed.

Divine Love *never* fails, but the important thing to realize is that Divine Love must be in your own heart and cannot operate from outside, so to speak. If you had sufficient Divine Love for everyone in your heart, you could heal others by speaking the Word once; and in many

---

3. See "Yoga of Love," and "Golden Gate," in *Power Through Constructive Thinking*, pp. 160 and 275.
4. First Epistle of John 4:16.
5. John 13:35.

cases your mere presence would bring about healing without your having made any special effort at all. Of course, by the time you reached this stage you would have gotten rid of all criticism and condemnation. You would never for an instant want to see someone punished or think "It serves him right." This does not mean you would condone wrong doing in any way, but you would condemn the wrong and not the wrong doer. If a small baby is troublesome or perhaps breaks a valuable object, you regret the act, but you do not hate the baby. So, in dealing with criminals and other delinquents, we should take whatever steps are wise concerning them, such as locking them up in humane prisons for their own good as well as that of society, but without hatred. A burglar must be restrained for instance not only to prevent his victims from being robbed but for his own sake, to prevent his criminal career developing and perhaps ultimately culminating in murder. Of course, his prison term should be reformatory and not just punitive.

In like manner you must not permit other people to cheat you or otherwise impose upon you. That would be to help them to be dishonest or selfish. Protect your own rights, but always in a spirit of Divine Love.

You probably know the old story of a stranger who settled in a town and asked his neighbor, "What are the people round here like?"

The neighbor, a Quaker, replied quietly with a question, "What were the people like where thee came from?"

The newcomer answered, "I have come from—. The people there were very mean and dishonest."

The Quaker answered, "I'm afraid thee will find them all here."

A third person who had overheard the conversation, joined in by remarking, "This surprises me because I have come from the same town, and I found them a very kind and friendly lot of people."

And the old Quaker, turning to him, said, "Thee will find them all here too."

To realize God as Love is the remedy for fear—and the only real one. Of late a great many books have been published on the subject of fear, but on examining them I find that in nearly all cases they only get as far as analyzing fear, saying what a bad thing it is and how much harm it does, and how important it is for us to get rid of it; but without offering any practical way of doing so. The truth is that there is only one remedy for fear, and that is to get some sense of Divine Love, by thinking about it, analyzing it, claiming it, and expressing it in practice toward all human beings without any exception.

If your prayers are not being answered, there must be something wrong. The universe is governed by law, and there is no such thing as a broken law. Jesus himself did not break the Law of Being when he performed his miracles; he could not, and he would not have wished to. He fulfilled the law when he prayed. When your prayers are not answered it must be because you have not fulfilled the conditions of the law, and, ninety-nine times in a hundred, it is because you are lacking in a sense of love for all. It is a cosmic law that Love heals and that fear and condemnation damage and destroy. Treat yourself for Love every day[6] and watch your thoughts, and watch your tongue, and watch your deeds, that nothing contrary to Love finds expression there.

Scientific Prayer consists in seeing God where the trouble seems to be. When a person seems to be behaving

---

6. See "Divine Love," in *Power Through Constructive Thinking*, p. 277.

badly, see the Presence of God in him. When a part of the body is sick or damaged, see the Presence of God there. Where there seems to be lack, see the Presence of God and claim Divine Love too, and when you *feel* the sense of Divine Love, your demonstration is made and what you need will come. You do not need to have a thrilling experience. That might be only psychic. A strong conviction of the Truth, with a sense of Divine Love, is what will demonstrate under all circumstances. You have a strong conviction that two and two make four, that Chicago is in Illinois, that the Statue of Liberty is in New York. You do not argue about these things, you just know them to be true. Have the same quiet, firm conviction about your statements of Truth, and you will demon-strate. Sometimes you get a beautiful sense of peace con-cerning the problem—the dove alights—but this does not have to happen in order to make your demonstra-tion. As a rule you will get it without that. If the dove alights, stop working.

Do not talk about your prayers; keep your spiritual business to yourself. Do not tell people that you are pray-ing for such and such a thing, or in such and such a way. Keep the affairs of your soul secret. When you get a demonstration do not run around and tell everyone about it immediately. Keep it to yourself until it has had time to crystallize, so to speak. When Jesus healed people, he said, "Go away and tell no one."

Because God is Love, God never punishes or threat-ens anyone. The action of God takes place only to heal and comfort and inspire. The nearer we get to God, the happier, more peaceful, and healthier we are. In fact, trouble and sickness are really the way in which we be-come aware that we have lost the sense of His Presence. When we make mistakes or do wrong, the punishment which we bring upon ourselves is the natural consequence of the law we have broken, and we shall continue to suffer until we cease to break the law. This is a wise arrangement and a very merciful one, for in no other way could we learn. A red hot stove burns your hand if you touch it. That is a good thing because if it did not you would some day inadvertently put your hand in the fire and it would be burnt off before you knew about it. God is Love, and God is the only power.

The FOURTH MAIN ASPECT of God is Intelligence. God is not merely intelligent but God is Intelligence itself. When you clearly realize that this is an intelligent universe it will make a major difference in your life. It is obvious that in an intelligent universe there cannot be any disharmony because all ideas must work together for the common good. This means that there can be no clashing or overlapping anywhere, and neither can there be any lack. An engine which has been intelligently designed does not have any unnecessary parts and neither are any essential parts lacking. The machine is just right, complete and perfect, and so is the universe when we understand it.

It is especially important to realize that God is Intelligence, for the following reason: It sometimes happens that when people outgrow the childish idea that God is just a magnified man, they go to the opposite extreme and think of God as merely a blind force, like gravity or electricity. This means that they have lost all sense of the Love and Fatherhood of God, and such an idea is very little better than a subtle form of atheism. Indeed, this standpoint is not very far removed from the attitude of the materialist who is usually a great believer in what he calls the laws of Nature.

In an intelligent universe there can be neither cruelty nor waste, for these two things are infallible symptoms of a lack of intelligence in those who are guilty of them. And so we know that inharmony and stupidity of any kind are but illusions of the carnal mind, and in fact they always begin to disappear under the realization of God as Intelligence.

Is God a person? No, God is not a person in the usual sense of the word. *God has every quality of personality except its limitation*. It is true that the human mind cannot imagine any personality which is not limited, but this difficulty arises from the very limitations of the human mind itself, and, of course, this does not affect the nature of God. The Bible says, in effect, whatever you think I am, that will I be to you; and this means that if we attribute to God every quality of an infinite, intelligent, loving personality, having infinite power, God will be just that to us. So we may say that we believe in a personal God, but not in an anthropomorphic God. There is nothing that an anthropomorphic God could be to us that the true God is not, and He is infinitely more besides.

In acquiring these wider and better ideas of God you should not feel that you have, so to speak, left the God of your childhood for a new God—as one might leave one political party and join a different one—but that you are simply getting a better and more adequate idea of the same God that you always worshiped; because, of course, there is only one God.

You should treat yourself for Intelligence at least two or three times a week, by thinking about it, and claiming it for yourself. This practice will make every activity of your life more efficient. There are sure to be some things that you could do in a better way than you are doing them, and this treatment will bring such things to your notice. If you are wasting time in certain directions this treatment will make the fact clear to you and you will be shown a better way of working. Some people are a little hurt at being told to treat themselves for Intelligence, regarding such advice as a reflection upon their mentalities, but the more really intelligent a person is the more he realizes how much more of that quality he needs.

When things in your life seem to be going wrong, treat yourself for Intelligence. When business or other conditions appear to have reached a deadlock, treat yourself for Intelligence. When you seem to be up against a stone wall and apparently there is no way out, treat yourself for Intelligence. If you have to deal with someone who is seemingly very stupid or foolish, realize that Divine Intelligence works in him because he is a child of God, and if you get sufficient realization he will change for the better. It may sometimes happen, however, that you are the person who was at fault, although you did not in the least suspect it, and in that case you will come to see it, and you yourself will change.

Children and young people respond very readily indeed to a treatment for Intelligence. If you are interested in a child at school or a young person at college, treat him several times a week for Intelligence and you will be surprised to find how his progress in his studies will increase.

Remember also the wonderful fact that when you treat a person (or yourself) spiritually, the result of that treatment will be with the patient not only in the present time, but for the rest of his life. If you treat little Johnny for Intelligence today, his school work will improve immensely, but fifty years from now when he is a man of sixty he will be more intelligent and therefore happier and more successful because of today's treatment.

If you are in business, treat yourself and your assistants for Intelligence several times a week. Some people make a practice of blessing the store or the office every morning soon after they arrive, and this brings splendid results.

The Intelligence Aspect of God is very important in its relation to the health of the body. It would not be an intelligent proceeding to make a body that can be easily hurt or damaged or one which would grow old after only seventy or eighty years' use; nor would it be intelligent to give to man faculties like sight or hearing which could begin to fail long before he had finished with them. Yet the carnal mind believes just these things, and so men's and women's bodies experience decay in what is called old age. Their ears, their eyes, and their teeth fail them and ultimately death comes. When the human race realizes clearly enough that God is Intelligence, the "old age belief" will be overcome.

We know that prayer is thinking about God, but in order to think about Him at all you must have a certain amount of knowledge of Him, and these Main Aspects furnish that. They enable us to think about God in an intelligent way. When you dwell upon one of these aspects you are developing that quality in yourself. When you think of that aspect as being in another person, you develop that quality in him. To think of God as Love makes you more loving, and gets rid of a certain amount of criticism, resentment, and condemnation. To think of God as Life improves your health and gives you more energy, and so forth. When some kind of trouble comes to you, try to realize the Main Aspect which represents the exact contrary. Thus you realize Love to overcome fear or anger, Life to heal sickness, Truth to uncover falsehood, and so forth.

The FIFTH MAIN ASPECT of God is Soul, and it is spelt with a capital S. Do not confuse this with the soul spelt with a small s, which is what modern psychology calls the psyche, and is another name for your human mind which consists of your intellect and your feelings.[7]

Soul is that Aspect of God by virtue of which He is able to *individualize* Himself. The word "individual" mans *un-divided* (see Webster). Most people seem to think that it means the exact contrary. It suggests separateness to them, but they are mistaken. Individual means undivided, and God has the power of *individualizing* Himself without, so to speak, breaking Himself into parts.

God individualizes Himself as man, and so you are really an individualization of God. God can individualize Himself in an infinite number of distinct beings, or units of consciousness, and yet not be in any way separate. Only God can do this because He is spirit. Matter cannot be individualized. It can only be broken up. Thus, if you were to tear off half a page of this book, and then tear that into small pieces you would have divided up the page. The remnant of the page would be smaller by the amount of paper torn off; and the whole page would be the sum of all the fragments. This is division; it is not individualization. Spirit, however, can be individualized, and this possibility is the Aspect of God that we call Soul.

This will be quite a new idea to most people (our customary training prepares us to understand matter only), and you should therefore think it over a good many times until you are satisfied that you really understand it.

---

7. See chapter, "The Four Horsemen of the Apocalypse."

So your real self, the Christ within, the spiritual man, the I Am, or the divine spark, as it is variously called, is an individualization of God. *You are the presence of God at the point where you are.* This does not, of course, mean that you are an absurd little personal God. You are an individualization of the one and only God.[8] Man may very well be compared to an electric light bulb.

The electric current is present in all parts of the circuit but it shines forth, or one might say, figuratively, becomes self-conscious, in the bulb.

So Divine Mind becomes self-conscious in you, and that is what you are. Jesus, who taught the people in a vine growing country, said, "I am the vine, ye are the branches."[9] Obviously the life in the branch is the common life of the whole vine expressed at that particular place, and if a branch is broken off from the parent vine it dies. Now, man cannot be separated from God in reality, but he can be separated in human belief, and when the belief in separation occurs, the belief in death follows in greater or lesser degree.[10] The lesser degrees are what we call sickness, depression, discouragement, and old age. In the greater degree it becomes the death belief itself, when we lose the body altogether and disappear from this plane, leaving the body behind. The death thought is actually an extremely acute charge of fear.

I would warn the reader that this is not a subject to be quickly mastered. Much rereading of this subject, and prayer for enlightenment, will be necessary to understand

---

8. John 10:34.
9. John 15:5.
10. See "The Good Shepherd," in *Power Through Constructive Thinking*, p. 47.

it thoroughly, and one should be on one's guard against jumping to rash conclusions.

To realize in some degree that you are an individualization of God could not possibly make you egotistic or vain. On the contrary, it would give you true humility and at the same time true self-confidence, and, indeed, it is the only pathway to the overcoming of fear.

Some of the ancient Egyptians spoke of man as a beam of the sun, and the same idea seems to have occurred to certain American aborigines. This is a wonderful idea and expresses the truth beautifully. If you will work regularly, realizing this oneness with God, you will change for the better out of all recognition. Your body and your mind will hardly be recognizable. People will say this cannot be you—it must be a younger brother, and how much finer he is than his senior! On the other hand, if you think negatively about yourself, if you believe that you are a miserable sinner and keep on saying so, that will be the best way to become one.

The Aspect of God as Soul is the one to realize when you are called upon to perform some task or undertake some responsibility that seems too great for you. For instance, a clerk in a business house may suddenly be called upon to take the manager's place, perhaps permanently, and he is frightened because he does not feel equal to it. Or on a ship at sea an inexperienced junior officer, owing to a chapter of accidents, may suddenly be called upon to take charge of the ship. In either case, the person concerned should work on the Aspect of God as Soul, realizing that he is an individualization of God and that therefore God works through him. If he gets this clear enough he will be amazed at how well everything will go, and he himself will have permanently entered a higher category of work.

When you realize that you are one with God, the task becomes "*Our* business" instead of "*my* business," because God is your partner. Of course, when you enter upon this partnership it is an essential part of the contract that you practice the Golden Rule. Everyone you deal with must get a square deal, which means treating him exactly as you would wish him to treat you if the positions were reversed.

The fingers of the great pianist are not in business for themselves, so to speak. His fingers are not independent, they are part of himself. They express him on the keys, and they do not have to bother to think which note they ought to strike or wonder if they will be able to do it. They know that they will find themselves striking the right notes, because the master plays through them or by means of them. God is God, and someone aptly said, "Man is the by-means-of."

The SIXTH MAIN ASPECT of God is Spirit. God is Spirit.[11] We know that God is Spirit but what does that mean? Well, Spirit is that which cannot be destroyed or damaged or hurt, or degraded or soiled in any way. Spirit cannot deteriorate. It cannot grow old or tired. It cannot know sin, or condemnation, or resentment, or disappointment. It is the opposite of matter. Matter is always deteriorating. While you sit reading this page, the book is actually wearing out. The clothes on your back are wearing out. The building in which you are sitting is wearing out, and your body itself is wearing out—and some day all these things will be dust. True, it will take a long time according to our ideas for these things to happen but happen they will. There was a time when great cities filled

---

11. John 4:24.

with imposing buildings and splendid monuments flourished in Africa and in Asia, cities of which every trace has now disappeared, for they have become one with the desert sands. This is inevitable because matter is always wearing out. "Cometh forth like a flower, and is cut down: fleeth also as a shadow, and continueth not."[12]

This is really a splendid thing because it means that the world is constantly being renewed. It is splendid that old things should disappear in order that newer, cleaner, and better things may take their place. If clothing did not wear out, many people would continue wearing it for many years until it became saturated with dirt, instead of which we get new clothes at frequent intervals. If automobiles did not wear out we might still be using the primitive models of thirty years ago. We should never try to hold on mentally to material objects, but be ever ready to renew and improve upon them. The chapter of Job quoted from above is an expression of the limited human view of these matters, the attitude of mind which was the real cause of Job's troubles.

Matter wears out, but Spirit does not because Spirit is *substance*. Herbert Spencer defines substance as that which is not subject to discord or decay. Webster says, "that which underlies all outward manifestation . . . real, unchanging essence or nature . . . that in which qualities inhere . . . that which constitutes anything what it is." All this can only apply to spiritual things.

You are Spirit. Your body is spiritual, but you are Spirit. Spirit cannot die and was never born. Your true self was never born and will never die. You are eternal, divine, unchanging Spirit, in your true nature. The whole universe is a spiritual creation but we see it in a limited way,

---

12. Job 14:2.

and that limited way we know as matter. You have sometimes seen a window made of fluted glass, and you know
that if you look at the street through this window everything will be distorted. The passers-by and the automobiles
will appear to be warped and distorted in absurd and ugly
ways. Nevertheless, you know that these things are really
quite right in themselves, and that the distortion arises
from your seeing them wrongly. So it is that damage,
decay, sin, sickness, and death, and all of what we call
"matter" arise from our false seeing. Our false vision causes
us to know ourselves only from a seeming birth to a seeming death; but this is illusion too. This distorted vision of
Spirit is really what we know as "matter." The Bible refers
to this distortion as the carnal mind. Eucken says, "Reality is an independent spiritual world, unconditioned by the
apparent world of sense"—and this is substance.

Matter is unreal in the philosophical sense. It is not, of
course, hallucination, but it is not the outer and separate thing that it seems to be. Life is a state of consciousness, and the world we see about us is part of our
consciousness. We are conscious of certain objects and
certain happenings, but these are mental experiences
though we unwittingly give them objective existence.

Material objects often seem to be very beautiful. The
beauty of nature and the beauty of art are familiar to all,
but such beauty is really Spirit or Truth shining through
and is not due to the matter. The thinner the veil of matter the more beauty do we see, and the thicker the veil of
matter the less beauty do we see. In a beautiful landscape
the veil of matter (the limitation in our thought) is comparatively thin, and in an ugly slum that veil is comparatively thick; but that is the only difference. All beauty, all
good, all joy, are the Presence of God apprehended
through the veil of matter.

The time to realize the Aspect of God as Spirit is when something seems to be damaged or soiled or in decay. If you can realize the presence of Spirit where the trouble seems to be the evil condition will begin to improve, and if your realization is sufficiently clear the condition will be completely healed.

When Jesus saw the man with the withered hand he realized that in Truth that hand was spiritual—and the hand was healed. When people said that Lazarus was dead, Jesus realized that true man is Spirit and dies not—and Lazarus came forth alive.

When you realize that any given thing is not in reality matter, but a spiritual idea seen in a limited way, that "thing" changes for the better. It matters not whether it be a living thing like a part of your body or an animal or a plant, or whether it is what we call an inanimate object, the law is the same. The so-called inanimate objects are really spiritual ideas. A table, a chair, your watch, your shoes, your house, the George Washington Bridge, are all spiritual ideas seen in the limited (clouded) way that we call matter. *You* are not a spiritual idea, you are an individualization of God, but things are spiritual ideas great or small. An animal is a wonderful grouping of God's ideas in which Intelligence is a principal component, but it is not an individualization.

If you find the last couple of pages difficult to follow, ignore them for the time being and study the rest of this chapter. Sooner or later you will see these things clearly for yourself. Do not theorize too much about this subject but try a few practical experiments. When something is giving trouble, affirm and try to realize that in reality it is a spiritual idea—and watch what happens. If an automobile, or any other kind of mechanism is giving trouble, try treating it. I know that this will sound fantastic to people unacquainted with spiritual law, and so I say, do not be obstinate but *try* it.

The SEVENTH MAIN ASPECT of God is Principle, and this is probably the one that is least understood. People do not usually think of God as Principle, but such He is. What does the word "principle" mean?

Well, consider a few generally accepted principles. "Water seeks its own level." This is a principle. It is not a particular drop of water and it is not the course taken by a particular drop of water in a particular locality, say the passage of a drop of water from the Ashokan Reservoir to your faucet in New York City. It is a general principle that is true of all water everywhere on earth. It is not a particular thing or a particular action. It is a principle.

Consider another principle: "Matter expands when heated." Because this is a principle it is true anywhere at any time under any circumstances. Heat a piece of steel and it will expand, no matter what country it is in, or who owns it, or for what purpose it is being used. This principle of expansion may help a piece of mechanism to run successfully, if the mechanism is well designed, or it may wreck it if it is not well designed, but the principle is unchanging. Again, this principle is not a thing or an action. It is not the steel nor is it the actual process of expansion; it is the fact that matter expands under heat.

Consider another principle: "The angles of any triangle always add up to 180°." It makes no matter what kind of triangle one may consider, as long as it *is* a triangle, this principle exists. Size or material makes no difference. The area of the triangle may be a square inch or a million square miles, the principle is the same. The triangle may be arranged horizontally, vertically, or in any plane, and the principle remains.

These principles, I repeat, were true a billion years ago and they will be true a billion years hence. They cannot and do not change, for a principle changes not.

God is the Principle of perfect harmony and God does not change, so perfect harmony is the nature of his creation. Prayer is answered because God is principle, and when we pray rightly we bring ourselves into harmony with the Law of Being. Scientific Prayer does not try to change the Law. It does not try to bring about exceptions in our favor. It does not ask God to change the laws of nature for our temporary convenience, but it tunes us in, so to speak, with Divine Principle; and then we find things coming right.

If you have a radio and you want to get the program on WJZ, you tune in for WJZ. You do not expect to get that program on WABC. As long as you are tuned to the wrong station, you do not expect the right program, and you do not beg God to change the programs about to suit you; nor do you weep or tear your hair. You alter the tuning of your set, until you are in synchronism with the station you want. We have problems and troubles because we

have tuned out mentally from God, or the Divine Principle of our being, and our only remedy is to tune back. If God were to make exceptions because we were in great difficulties (which, because of His nature, He could never do) we should never know where we stood. If the law of gravity did not work at certain times, say on Tuesdays, or if it were occasionally suspended without notice, say, because a very important man had fallen off a roof, you know what would happen to the world. Apart from anything else, we should be left in confusion because we should never know what to expect; but the law of gravity never does cease to operate, because it is a principle.

You may be inclined to think that this fact is limiting, or even depressing, but on the contrary it is extremely encouraging because, since principle cannot change, you know that you must always make your demonstration if only you can rise high enough in consciousness. If you should raise your consciousness and yet not get your healing or your freedom it could only mean that Principle had broken down—but you know that that cannot happen, and so it is only a question of enough prayer or treatment, and your difficulty, whatever it is, must yield.

God is Principle, the Principle of perfect harmony, and therefore *perfect harmony is the Law of Being*. You should note that this sentence is in itself a very powerful treatment.

This Aspect of God, namely, Principle, may be used at any time, but it is especially helpful when you are feeling discouraged about your prayers, and in cases where there seems to be a great deal of ill feeling or prejudice involved. In other cases where there seems to be any sense of vindictiveness or spite, such things will melt away under the realization that Divine Principle is the only power that exists, and that there simply is no false personality to think evil of that kind.

These are the Seven Main Aspects of God and we have considered them separately, one at a time, but, of course, God has them all, all the time, and one cannot really draw a hard and fast line between them. To take an example, we know that the rose, for instance, has color—red. It has weight—so many grams. It has shape. It has fragrance—an odor. Here are four different things, color, weight, shape, and fragrance; and we determine them and talk about them separately, in order thoroughly to

understand the rose; but the rose has them all at the same
time and all the time. So these Seven Main Aspects are all
true of God at all times. In practice it is often better to handle a particular problem by realizing two or more of them.
In case of doubt, quietly claim that God is thinking
through you. *God thinks by means of man—God thinks through
me,* is one of the best affirmations you can use at any time.

Each of the Seven Main Aspects is a distinct quality
like the elements in chemistry. A chemical element, as
you know, is just itself and nothing else. Oxygen is an element because there is nothing in it but oxygen. Hydrogen is an element, for there is nothing in it but
hydrogen. Water on the other hand is a compound, a
combination of hydrogen and oxygen; and so are steel
and sulphuric acid compounds, to take other examples.
There are many attributes of God, such as wisdom, beauty,
joy, and so forth, but they are compounds, made up of two
or more of the Seven Main Aspects. Wisdom, for example, is the perfect balance of Intelligence and Love. It is
not an element. If you had Intelligence without Love,
you could, for a time at least, have cleverly organized
wickedness. The traditional Satan is an example of such
a case. He is always credited with being extremely intelligent in promoting his schemes. Again, when you have
Love without Intelligence, you can have boundless folly.
The spoilt child is the most obvious example of this danger. The parent is full of Love but is lacking in Intelligence, and so he spoils the child and makes him a
nuisance to himself and all those around him.

Beauty is an attribute of God and is the perfect balance of Life, Truth, and Love. In any true work of art,
be it a picture, a building, a musical composition, or what
you please, you will find that these three Aspects are balanced. One often comes across a work of art which he

admires, but he feels that it somehow misses being complete; and a careful analysis will show that one of these Aspects is missing, or is not sufficiently represented.

In a sense it may be said that the first three Aspects are the most fundamental, and they are represented by the three primary colors, yellow for Life, blue for Truth, and red for Love. This is not an arbitrary arrangement, but has a metaphysical basis, and if you are interested in this phase of the Truth you can follow it up by treating for inspiration on the subject.

When you realize that the whole universe is but a network of thoughts and that actually man can know nothing but his own states of mind, you will see that there must be all kinds of unsuspected relationships and interdependencies between seemingly unrelated things in the outer world—"Thou canst not pluck a flower without the trembling of a star."

There are two synonyms for the word God—Mind and Cause. These are not "Aspects" of God but are synonyms. Each means exactly the same as the word God itself. God is the religious name for the Creator of all things. Mind is the metaphysical name, and Cause is the natural science name for God. Anything that has any real existence is an idea in the One Mind; and this is the metaphysical interpretation of the universe. From the natural science point of view we may say that all creation is the result or effect of One Cause (God), and that there are no secondary causes. Now a cause cannot be known directly. It can be known only by its effect, and so the universe is the manifestation or effect of Cause or God, and because God is good, it must be good too.

Think over these Main Aspects every day. If you are a quick thinker go over these several times. If you are a slow thinker go through them once or twice. There is no special advantage in being either a quick or a slow thinker, it is a matter of natural temperament and one can accomplish just as much work as the other. Claim that you understand each one of them and that you express it. An excellent practice is to use the Divine Love Card for each Aspect, changing the word "Love" to whichever Aspect you are working on at the moment.

Make Your Life Worthwhile

H AVE you ever realized that all around us there lies a realm of infinite power which we can train ourselves at any time to tap for our own use? This power surrounds us as the atmosphere does, and, like the atmosphere, it belongs to everyone, and is at the disposal of anyone, for any good purpose. This Power, which is the real source of all things that exist, needs only to be consciously contacted in order to flow into your being, and transform itself into health, into true prosperity, into inspiration, or into anything else that you may be needing. This Power is quite impersonal in itself, but it is always seeking a chance to express itself through particular personalities, through you or through me, if only we will let it.

We all do let it do so at times, but only very rarely in most cases. Without in the least understanding what we are doing, we—once in a blue moon at least—give that power a chance to "come through," and then we say that we have a splendid idea, we do not know from where; or that we are feeling so wonderfully well today, we do not know why, but we have gotten through about three times as much work as usual; or everything seems to be going right just now; or we have had such a wonderful piece of "luck." Now what has really happened in these cases is that, for one reason or another, we have happened to contact the Universal Power for a short time.

But there is really no reason at all why we should not learn to contact this Power at any time, whenever we want to, and not just very occasionally and by chance. There is no reason why we should not train ourselves to allow it to work for us—or rather through us—every day in the week. There is no reason why we should not allow it to build up strong, healthy, and beautiful bodies for us. There is no reason why we should not allow it to over- come our difficulties, wipe out our mistakes—because it can do that too—furnish us with new and original ideas for our work or our home; why, in fact, we should not make it possible for that Power to make our lives into the beautiful and joyous things that Providence intended them to be.

In other words, there is no reason why every man and woman should not become what is usually called a ge- nius—a genius of any kind, either in natural science, or literature, or art, or music, or engineering, or business. Make no mistake about business. Business needs genius just as much as do any of the arts. A man who obtains new and practical ideas, and builds up a great successful business organization, serving the public, and finding employment for many people, is just as much a national asset as is a genius in any other walk of life.

What we have usually been accustomed to call a ge- nius is a man or woman who *happens* to have this faculty of contacting the "Great Universal Power." My point, how- ever, is that it is possible, and not even very difficult, for the ordinary person, once he has become aware of the possibility, to begin to contact that Power consciously, and gradually to transform himself into a genius.

Many people have always felt in a vague sort of way that something of this kind might be possible in the Fine Arts, but now I want to stress the fact that the great Life Power is just as ready to help us in what we are pleased to call the prosaic, everyday affairs of our lives. The reason for this is that from the point of view of that Universal Power, nothing *is* prosaic, or pretty, or mean, so long as it concerns the lives of men and women. Emerson said, "Man's welfare is dear to the heart of Being," and that is quite true. The great Universal Power is always ready to come into your life—if you will invite it—to solve whatever problem may be important to you; to overcome for you the difficulty that is worrying you, even if that difficulty should seem to be rather a trifling thing to someone who is not concerned with your welfare.

Right now I have a case in mind of a woman who has for some time been making a handsome income as a dress designer. Her ideas are so original and so good that she has no trouble at all in commanding very high fees. She loves her work, and she would not change places, she says, with any man or woman on earth. Yet, only a few years ago she was in great poverty and, apparently, there was no way for her to provide for herself and her mother who was dependent upon her. Then she began each day to set aside a certain time for becoming quiet—withdrawing her attention from outer things and inviting the Power to lead and inspire her with the necessary guidance, out of what seemed to be a hopeless blind-alley.

She told me that she did not find this an easy thing to do for the first few days; because she was so worried by the creditors who were pressing her that it seemed very difficult to stop thinking about her troubles, even for a few minutes. She knew that it was absolutely necessary to do so, however, and she succeeded after the first few attempts, with the result that she first of all experienced a remarkable change in feeling. The worry and fear went first, and then she became aware of a sense of power and adequacy to cope with her problems. The day after this happened, when she was thinking of something quite different, the thought of a certain business acquaintance suddenly flew into her mind as though, she says, someone had thrown it at her, like a snowball. She felt satisfied that this inspiration had come, not from "herself" but from "It," meaning the Great Universal Power of intelligence and wisdom. She went straight off to the person in question, and to her intense surprise, received an offer, there and then, which, at that time, was a very attractive one for her. She thought she knew very little about dress designing, but she decided to put that problem, too, up to the Universal Power. She continued each day to contact the Power in the same way, and day by day the difficulties as they arose were easily overcome. Then she began to go to the same Source for original ideas to use in her work. Remember that with her all this had been very much of an experiment—and when original ideas began to arrive, too, her career was made.

A certain architect, a very successful man, noted for the originality and brilliance of his work, is in the habit of working in very much the same way. In his case it was an original discovery. No one told him about it—he stumbled upon it for himself.

There is another case of a well-known lawyer, famous for his brilliant work in court, who owes his success, he says, almost entirely to contacting the Great Power in

very much this way. He has said that he not only got some
"hunches" of vital importance in this way, enabling him
to handle very difficult cases, but his health, which had
seemed to be the principal obstacle to a successful career, was completely restored by the influx of power which
he received during these contacts with the Great Universal Energy. This is his firm opinion, and I suppose
that he ought to know.

This Power, this Energy is there. It is universal, which
means that it is present everywhere. It belongs to nobody
in particular because it belongs to all. It is waiting at all
times for men and women to call it out into use for any
good purpose in life. The fact that most people do not suspect its existence does not change the fact that it is there.
Remember that hardly anyone except one or two philosophers suspected the existence of the atmosphere, or of
electricity, or of the power of steam, until a few generations ago; and now these things have been brought into
the service of man and have transformed the world. The
wonderful things they have given us, such as the telephone, the airplane, the automobile, could have been
had hundreds or thousands of years ago just as well, because the laws of Nature were just the same then as they
are now; only people did not know that such forces existed and so they had to go without. Today the knowledge of the existence of this supreme force is being given
to the people, and before very long, I believe, many of the
limitations and difficulties that people take for granted
at present, will be things of the past.

Now I am going to suggest that those of you who are interested in this article should make an experiment for
yourselves. Do not waste any time in arguing about
whether the thing sounds reasonable or not, but try it
out for yourself. Get by yourself for a few minutes once

a day for several days—if you can choose about the same time each day, so much the better, but this is not essential—drop all your worries for the time being—this *is* absolutely essential—relax the body, and quietly invite the Great Universal Power to come into your mind and endow you with whatever thing you are most needing; whether that be health, or guidance, or some information concerning a particular matter, or a job, or even money, or what not. But on no account must you give instructions to that Power, because it will not take them; and if you try to compel it, nothing will happen. Be receptive. Be open-minded. Be humble. Do not be impatient; and you will see what you will see. Something remarkable will happen.

How to Get a Demonstration

H ERE is one way of solving a problem by Scientific Prayer, or, as we say in metaphysics, of getting a demonstration.

Get by yourself, and be quiet for a few moments. This is very important. Do not strain to think rightly or to find the right thought, etc., but just be quiet. Remind yourself that the Bible says *Be still, and know that I am God.*

Then begin to think about God. Remind yourself of some of the things that you know about Him—that He is present everywhere, that He has all power, that He knows you and loves you and cares for you, and so forth. Read a few verses of the Bible, or a paragraph from any spiritual book that helps you.

During this stage it is important not to think about your problem, but *to give your attention to God*. In other words, do not try to solve your problem directly (which would be using will power) but rather become interested in thinking of the Nature of God.

Then claim the thing that you need—a healing, or some particular good which you lack. Claim it quietly and confidently, as you would ask for something to which you are entitled.

Then give thanks for the accomplished fact, as you would if somebody handed you a gift. Jesus said when you pray believe that you receive and you shall receive.

Do not discuss your treatment with anyone.

Try not to be tense or hurried. *Tension and hurry delay the demonstration.* You know that if you try to unlock a door hurriedly, the key is apt to stick, whereas, if you do it slowly, it seldom does. If the key sticks, the thing is to stop pressing, take your breath, and release it gently. To push hard with will power can only jam the lock completely. So it is with all mental working.

In quietness and confidence shall be your strength.

Keep on the Beam

T ODAY most commercial flying is done on a radio beam. A directional beam is produced to guide the pilot to his destination, and as long as he keeps on this beam he knows that he is safe, even if he cannot see around him for fog, or get his bearings in any other way.

As soon as he gets off the beam in any direction he is in danger, and he immediately tries to get back on to the beam once more.

Those who believe in the All-ness of God, have a spiritual beam upon which to navigate on the voyage of life. As long as you have peace of mind and some sense of the Presence of God you are on the beam, and you are safe, even if outer things seem to be confused or even very dark; but as soon as you get off the beam you are in danger.

You are off the beam the moment you are *angry* or *resentful* or *jealous* or *frightened* or *depressed;* and when such a condition arises you should immediately get back on the beam by turning quietly to God in thought, claiming

His Presence, claiming that His Love and Intelligence are with you, and that the promises in the Bible are true today. If you do this you are back on the beam, even if outer conditions and your own feelings do not change immediately. You are back on the beam and you will reach port in safety.

Keep on the beam and nothing shall by any means hurt you.

The Magic of Tithing

S O many inquiries have recently been made upon the subject of tithing, and so much confusion appears to exist in people's minds concerning it, that it seems that a few notes on the matter will be generally useful at the present time.

The practice of tithing has been a life-long habit with many Truth students. So much has it become a regular part of the scheme of things for them that they naturally think of their own money as amounting to 90 percent of whatever their net income happens to be. Automatically they set aside the 10 percent that belongs to God, nor ever dream of breaking into it. This they do intelligently, that is to say, on principle, and for the sole reason that they have perceived it to be the right and proper course. The unfailing result of this is that such people are always free from financial difficulties. Though they may have other problems, they are never in want, or lacking in material prosperity. They fulfill the law, and so they inevitably demonstrate the result.

This fact is becoming widely known at the present day, but what seems not to be so generally understood is the true Spiritual Principle underlying it. One receives all sorts of questions about how tithing should be done—in what circumstances it should or should not be practiced; what money should and should not be tithed; in what manner the tithe should be apportioned; whether the practice of tithing really is an infallible recipe for getting rich; and so on.

The truth about tithing is that those who set aside 10 percent of their net incomes to the service of God—not with the primary motive of getting, but simply because they feel that it is right to do it—do find that their prosperity increases by leaps and bounds, until all fear of poverty disappears; whereas those who tithe because in their hearts they look upon it as a good investment, expecting or hoping to get back much more than they give, are certain to be disappointed, and are, from their point of view, wasting their money.

The practice of tithing is definitely prescribed in numerous places in the Bible, and in all ages there have been many believers in the true God who have made this habit the cornerstone of their lives—and have built upon that cornerstone an edifice of prosperity which insured them that freedom from material cares that is so essential to the development of the soul.

"Bring ye all the tithes into the storehouse, that there may be meat in mine house, and prove me now herewith, saith the Lord of hosts, if I will not open you the windows of heaven, and pour you out a blessing, that there shall not be room enough to receive it" (Malachi 3:10).

It is common knowledge that many of the most successful business men of the present day, great industrialists, Captains of Industry, as they are called, attribute their success, and rightly, to having formed this habit in youth and maintained it. Thousands of Truth students have grown out of longstanding, and what looked like hopeless poverty, into security and comfort by the practice of tithing, and thousands more are doing so at the present time.

"And all the tithe of the land, whether of the seed or the land, or of the fruit of the tree, is the Lord's: it is holy unto the Lord" (Leviticus 27:30).

"Honor the Lord with thy substance, and with the first fruits of thine increase: So shall thy barns be filled with plenty, and thy presses shall burst out with new wine" (Proverbs 3:9, 10).

Jacob, after he had received the vision which told him that there is a mystical ladder reaching from earth to heaven—the ladder of Scientific Prayer and righteous activity—decided there and then to adopt the practice of tithing, realizing that—

"God will be with me, and will keep me in this way that I go, and will give me bread to eat, and raiment to put on, so that I come again to my father's house in peace."

The secret of demonstrating prosperity in the spiritual way—and on no other basis can your prosperity ever be secure—is to understand, that is, to know to the point of realization, that the one and only source of your supply is God, and that your business or employment, your investments, your clients or customers, are but the particular channel through which that supply is at the moment coming to you from God. Now the practice of tithing with the right, that is to say the spiritual, motive, is really the concrete proof that you have accepted this position, and the invariable consequence of that acceptance is prosperity. It is quite easy now to see the difference between this, the spiritual practice, and the material and useless practice of putting aside the tenth part, often grudgingly, in the hope of making a good investment. As an expression of what is felt to be spiritual justice, tithing is an inevitable success; as a selfish investment, it is doomed to failure.

The principle of tithing having been accepted, the question arises as to what should be done with it. As tithing is understood in Divine Science, it does not include general charity or material giving. It is devoted to the spreading abroad of the knowledge of Truth in some form or other, usually in support of those institutions or activities which are thus employed. Anyone who understands the Spiritual Idea, knows that the one and only thing that the world needs to deliver it from its difficulties is knowledge of Spiritual Truth; that until a man comes to this knowledge, no other thing will really benefit him; that until this knowledge becomes general, no amount of secular learning, no scientific discoveries, no schemes of social reform, no amount of political reconstruction, can do any real good; and that once this knowledge does become general, all political and social problems will adjust themselves automatically, and all forms of charity and patronage become unnecessary. We know that by virtue of possessing the knowledge of the Truth of Being, we are nothing less than trustees for humanity. Those who are without this knowledge will continue to donate their money to the promotion of general good works, but we know that our first duty is the dissemination of Truth—

"Ye shall know the Truth, and the Truth shall make you free."

The fixing of the amount of the tithe is a very simple matter. It does not, as one student supposed, mean a tenth of the amount which he found himself able to save out of his income each month. It means a tenth of the whole income. A merchant will naturally deduct the expenses of his business before writing his net profit, but it is upon the whole of the net profit before any personal or living expenses are subtracted, that he would assess his tithe. People working for a salary receive their net income direct in that form, but they would naturally add to it any dividends that they might get from investments, and so on.

Needless to say, there is not the least obligation upon anyone to tithe at all until he reaches the state of consciousness when he will prefer to do so. In fact, it is better that he should not attempt to do so until he is ready. To give grudgingly or with misgivings from a supposed sense of duty, is really to give from a sense of fear, and no prosperity ever came out of fear.

On the other hand, the payment of a tithe is an extremely efficient act of Faith. It often happens that the student of Divine Science wholeheartedly desires to put his trust really in God, to possess scientific faith. Now, to desire this wholeheartedly is to have it. Yet he cannot always at first secure a sense of stabilized conviction, and because he cannot experience this feeling, he is apt to think himself lacking in faith when in reality he is not. But if he practices tithing as a result of an honest conviction that it is the right thing to do, that will be the proof of his faith, irrespective of what his feelings may tell him at the moment.

Some think that because they are in pressing difficulties it is impossible for them to tithe at the present time, but they propose to do so as soon as circumstances improve. This is to miss the whole point—the greater the present necessity, the greater the need for tithing, for we know that the present difficulties can only be due to one's mental attitude (probably subconscious) and that circumstances cannot improve until there is a change in the mental attitude. True spiritual tithing will be an indication that this attitude is changing, and will be followed by the desired demonstration. Tithing being on the percentage basis, the less one has, the less he gives, and so that problem adjusts itself.

The answer to the question of how often a tithe should be paid is quite simple. The correct time to pay it is upon the receipt of the income, whether that be monthly, weekly, half-yearly, and so on. In a general way, it is better to pay small sums frequently than larger sums more rarely, but here no definite rule can be given.

"Give, and it shall be given unto you; good measure, pressed down, shaken together, and running over, shall men give into your bosom. For with the same measure that ye mete withal it shall be measured to you again" (Luke 6:38).

Many Truth teachers have testified to the unfailing benefits of tithing. John Murray wrote:

> According to Hebrew Law, tithes means tenths, and refers to a form of taxation, which, under the Levitical Law, required the Hebrews to render a certain proportion (one-tenth) of the produce of the earth, herds, etc., to the service of God. And it is noteworthy, that as long as this system prevailed, the Hebrew Nation prospered, collectively and individually, and wherever it has been tried honestly and faithfully, it has never failed. If the farmer should refuse to give back to the soil a certain percentage of the corn and potatoes which the soil has given to him, he would have no crops.

Why, then, should we expect to receive Abundance from God, and give back so niggardly to His Holy cause. . . . Those who tithe are always certain that they have God for a partner.[1]

The connection between tithing and prosperity is, after all, but a particular expression of the general law that what we are to the universe, that will the universe be to us; that what we give out, whether it be generosity or parsimony, that we shall receive back; that like attracts like; that whatsoever a man soweth, that shall he also reap; and that no man escapes the Law.

---

1. *The Gleaner*, November, 1922.

How to Maintain Peace

I S it not a wonderful thought that you, perhaps an undistinguished and unknown, everyday person, can sit quietly in your room and do more to save the world from the inconceivable horrors of another war than can all the statesmen and diplomats put together? Yet, such is the case.

Many people are speaking today as though another war were inevitable. Others, on the contrary, declare optimistically that such a thing is impossible. The actual fact is that another war is neither inevitable nor impossible. There can be another war (and if there is, the destructions and horrors entailed will eclipse anything dreamed of up to the present, owing to the extraordinary advance of natural science and engineering in the past two decades), and such an event would almost certainly be the end of Western Civilization as we have known it.

On the other hand, there is not the least necessity for another war. It could happen, but it is not *necessary*. There is at hand a means by which a comparatively small number of people, if they so desire, can prevent war from breaking out. In this essay I intend to show exactly how that can be done.

To understand intelligently the problem that we have to face, we need to inquire why war ever does break out. Most people suppose that a war occurs as the result of certain definite acts on the part of certain individuals. They think that National leaders in a position of authority decide to make war on a neighbor because they feel that they are strong enough to conquer him; or that they declare war in self-defense with the object of forestalling such an attack upon themselves. Or it may be that they are drawn into a war already in progress between their neighbors, in spite of all efforts to keep out. This is the common view of history; but it is, however, quite wrong. The fact is that the concrete acts of individuals, such as ultimatums, declarations of war, and so forth, are never in themselves causal, but are merely the results of wide and deep currents of thought and feeling already existing in the masses of the peoples concerned. War breaks out between two countries because, for a long time beforehand, the hearts of thousands of people on both sides of the frontier have been filled with hatred and fear, and sometimes also with greed, satanic pride, and the rest of the Seven Deadly Sins. The war itself, and all the horrors that go with it—the shooting and bayoneting, the maiming and gassing, the destruction of property, and so forth— are but the aftermath or outpicturing on the physical plane of the evil passions which preceded it.

It is not possible for an act of violence to take place in the outer world of experience unless there is first a thought of violence (fear, hatred, etc.) in the inner world of thought. And it is equally true that it is not possible for thoughts of violence to hold sway in men's souls without being sooner or later enacted in the outer.

It naturally follows from this that the scientific method for the prevention of war must lie in the changing of the mentality of the people; and there is no other way. But how is this mental change to be brought about? Can it be done by the educational efforts of books and pamphlets, the holding of peace meetings, the convening of international conferences, and so forth? Well, all these things are efforts in the right direction, of course, but it has to be admitted that their practical results are usually very meager and out of proportion to the expense and effort involved. We know that all recent wars were preceded by efforts of this kind, which, nevertheless, completely failed to prevent them. Nay, there is a very definite danger lurking among these good intentions, because many spiritually-minded people are lulled into a false sense of security by trusting in them.

There is, however, a method of preventing war which is both simple in its application and unfailing in its results. It costs absolutely nothing to apply, and it can be put into effect by anyone, anywhere, who is prepared to give a little time to it. That method is Scientific Prayer.

If even a comparatively small number of people will learn to pray *scientifically*, and will then devote even a few minutes *daily* to Scientific Prayer for universal peace *there will never be another war.* Of course, it goes without saying that there are more than enough men and women of good will in the world ready to do this, and the only problem is to teach them how.

Let me say here that I cannot too strongly emphasize the fact that it must be *Scientific Prayer* if it is to be of any practical use. Other methods of prayer, while excellent in their own time and place for other purposes, are of little practical use for the prevention of war. They will comfort the individual, purify and develop his soul, and arm him with fortitude to meet his troubles; but they will not prevent war. Only *Scientific Prayer* will do that—and that it will do it is beyond any question. It is only necessary that enough people (and not a very large number numerically) should pray in the right way, and war will not come.

But what is Scientific Prayer? Scientific Prayer may be briefly described as the Practice of the Presence of God. In order to prevent war, you should devote at least five minutes a day to the realization of the Presence of God in all the peoples constituting the half dozen Great Powers. Do not work in this way for the whole of humanity, but only for the peoples of what are called the Great Powers, as it is desirable to concentrate the work where it is needed. War will not come unless some of the Great Powers become involved.

You may begin your prayer by reading a few verses of the Bible, or any spiritual book that appeals to you, or by repeating a favorite hymn or spiritual poem. Then declare that God is everywhere, and that all men, in Absolute Truth, are now spiritual and perfect, expressing only Love, and Wisdom, and Intelligence. That, in Reality there are no separate nations, because all men belong to the One Nation, the Divine Family. That there are no frontiers because God is One, and cannot be separated against Himself. That in Truth the only armaments are the forces of Love and Intelligence.

Then declare that God is fully present in every man, woman, and child in Britain, France, Germany, Italy, Japan, Russia, and the United States,[1] and that they can only know and express Serene Peace, Divine Intelligence, and Divine Love. To do this is to concentrate the work

---

1. Taking them alphabetically.

where it is needed and will be effective. You may conclude by giving thanks to God for the glory of His Own Divine Perfection, which never can change. If you wish to go on longer, use one of the last half dozen Psalms, all of which deal with praise and thanksgiving.

Having finished your prayer or treatment, drop the subject out of your mind until next day. It will be seen that this prayer is exclusively concerned with a realization of good. On no account must you allow yourself to dwell upon the horrors of war, the danger of war, or the causes of war, or think about war under any pretext whatever during the treatment. In fact, the whole prayer or treatment in itself is nothing but an effort to get away in thought from the concept of war. To say something like this—"Please God, do not allow another terrible war to happen," is to think of war, even though it sounds pious and edifying, and to think of a thing is to help to create or perpetuate that thing.

War must come as long as the thoughts that produce war remain in the human heart. A meditation or treatment of the scientific kind will have the effect of clearing that war thought out of the race mind, and then war will not come.

Understand clearly that you are not asked to maintain this uplifted state of mind all day long, but only for the few minutes that you are praying. Of course, you will, in a general way, avoid dwelling upon horrors at any time, for your own sake; but, provided you get right away from them during the period of prayer, you will have done all that is necessary to prevent war.

With regard to the length of time that should be devoted to this work each day, it may be said that mere length of time is unimportant; it is the degree of realization that counts. If you can get away in thought from the sense of limitation and war danger in two minutes, that will do. If it takes you half an hour to do so, you must give that. <u>Do not keep on too long on any one day. Some people will make little progress for several weeks, and then gradually find it coming easy. The one thing that matters is to get away, even for a moment, from the sense of fear and danger.</u> That will definitely and positively change the mentalities of the people in the countries concerned, and will prevent war.

Be faithful to this daily prayer. Unstable people usually start off such a plan by praying too long for several days, and then, having grown tired of it, drop it altogether. One is praying too long when he gets a sense of burden and fatigue. <u>Five minutes a day will do for most people. Remember that the joy of the Lord is your strength. This practice will bring a great blessing into your own life</u>.

Meditation for Peace

God is the only real presence and the only real power. God is fully present at every point of existence. God works through man, who is part of the Divine Expression. God works through all men indiscriminately, and in His sight there are no distinctions of nationality or party, and no frontiers. Therefore there can be no strife. With One God there can be only one plan, God's perfect plan, and all men are part of that; so each has his own place in the Divine Scheme, and there can be no competition or strife. God is all in all, and in Him all men live and move and have their being in perfect harmony and Love.

The American Spirit*

The Principles Underlying the Constitution

"No weapon that is formed against thee shall prosper; and every tongue that shall rise against thee in judgment thou shalt condemn. This is the heritage of the servants of the Lord, and their righteousness is of me, saith the Lord."

ISAIAH 54:17

T HE United States is not merely one more nation added to the list of nationalities. It stands for certain special ideas and special principles which have never been definitely expressed in concrete form in the world before. These ideas may be summed up in the conception of personal freedom and unlimited opportunity.

What may be called the American Spirit is an intangible though very real thing in itself, but as far as it can be put into words it has been expressed in the two great official documents of the American Republic, namely, the Constitution and the Declaration of Independence.

---

*Originally published in 1939.

These two documents are among the most remarkable ever written, and their effect upon the history of the world has probably never been surpassed. They are both quite short, not more than a few thousand words in length, but every thoughtful man anywhere, and certainly every American, should make himself acquainted with them. They can be easily obtained, well printed and bound up together, for about ten cents.[1] So there is no excuse for not being familiar with their contents.

The first thing that strikes us in considering these documents is the remarkable difference in their approach to the subject. The Constitution contains no direct preaching at all. It makes no direct statements about the nature of man or his destiny, or of man's relations with other people or with God. It is, seemingly, just a dry legal document. Never does it say in so many words that man should be free, that human beings should live together in brotherhood, or that man is the child of God. All these things are expressed or implied in the Declaration of Independence; and the Declaration is, I suppose, one of the most vivid and colorful documents that have ever been written. It thrills with hope and faith and enthusiasm. The Constitution, on the other hand, is formal, technical, precise, and not, at first sight, of any interest to the layman. Indeed, the Constitution and the Declaration might be described, in a sense, as the anatomy and physiology of government—the one concerned with the hard dry bones of the supporting skeleton, and the other with the warm living organs and tissues of life.

To understand the American Constitution one must realize that it aims at bringing about a definitely selected condition of things. It aims at a special way of life—a way

---

1. Rand McNally, Chicago.

of life that up to the present has only been found in completeness in the United States. It aims at *personal freedom* for the individual. It aims at the idea of substantial equality, and, above all, at equality of opportunity. No civilization had ever before aimed at that. The great Roman Empire had certain magnificent aims, but equality of opportunity was not one of them. The Greek civilization had wonderful aims, but they did not include that. Glorious Athens was always based on a foundation of slavery. The Middle Ages definitely rejected the idea of personal freedom and equality of opportunity, and aimed rather at discipline and uniformity.

America is the land of opportunity. This is an old saying, but it is still as true today as it ever was. An American said to me the other day that, while this statement might have been true at one time, he thought that it was no longer the case. He was wrong, however. The saying is just as true today as it ever was, as I hope to show in this essay. It is true that the western frontier has been closed for more than forty years, but the frontiers of scientific discovery and creative imagination can never be closed. And, as long as a people possesses individual freedom and equality of opportunity, these things will provide careers for all.

America is the land of opportunity. I myself have spent practically all my life in Europe, and so I come to American institutions and American conditions with a fresh mind; and the longer I live in America, the more I realize the substantial freedom that is here. In France and in England there is much political freedom, and there is personal freedom in many ways too—more political freedom in England than in France, and perhaps more personal freedom in France than in England. But, even in these countries, freedom is still limited in many ways

unknown to Americans. In all the old countries, owing to
their inheritance of the Feudal System,[2] there are all sorts
of *invisible* barriers to the free expression of the soul of
man, which is part of the self-expression of God. These
barriers are invisible. If they were visible the people would
get angry and tear them down, but they are invisible, and
they are nonetheless real for that.

In the United States, as one goes up and down the
land and meets all sorts of people, he realizes that these
invisible, and often very cruel, barriers do not exist here.
I have taken the trouble to study this subject as well as I
could. I have been in every state in the Union, and I have
talked these things over with every kind of person. I have
had the privilege of talking with some of the most distinguished people in America—with prominent statesmen, with some of our leading professional men, and
with important industrial executives. I have also talked
with working-men—with locomotive engineers, and with
soldiers and sailors and policemen. In the course of my
travels from the Atlantic to the Pacific and from Canada
to Mexico, I have talked with New Englanders, with South-
erners from the deep South, and with people from the
Middle West. I have talked with cowboys on the plains
and with prospectors and miners in the Rockies, and I
have been all over California and Texas. I have talked
with Negro laborers in the South and with highly educated Negroes in Harlem, and with Indians on the reser-
vation; and, I think, with almost every kind of person
that goes to make up the United States.

As I say, I have had the privilege of discussing just
these questions with some very important people, and
with many everyday people—the people one strikes up

---

2. See chapter 17, "The Historical Destiny of the United States."

an acquaintance with at hot dog stands by the roadside, in dining wagons, drug stores, and village groceries. And I can be a good listener when I want to, and they have told me, each in his own idiom, what they thought about the things and the ideas that were moving them at the time. And so I think I know something of the conditions of life in the United States today. I think I know something of what I am talking about; and I am constantly struck by two things in this country: The first thing that strikes me is the personal freedom, and the richness of opportunity which is here in normal times. The second thing that strikes me is that most Americans take it all so much for granted, that, in a sense, they appreciate it so little. I know that they do appreciate it, but not, I think, as they should. They say, "How else would it be?" But I tell you that without the Constitution it could be and would be very different, because these conditions are simply not known in any other country. They never have been known anywhere else. Only in the United States is general personal freedom and equality of opportunity an accepted thing. And it is the object of this essay to help people to realize this.

On the subject of opportunity I am constantly amazed by the evidence which I find of the wealth of opportunity for the average man or woman. The country is just coming out of a nine year panic of belief in depression; but, in normal times, it is hardly possible that an industrious man should not find opportunity to rise to any level in America.

Some months ago, speaking on a public platform in New York, I asked the people to send me data of cases known to them personally, of men and women who had risen to the top in their own fields *without any influence*— without any of those invisible elevators and private roads that are so general in the older countries. I repeated the request in a radio broadcast a week or so later, and the response on both occasions was so large, I received so many authenticated examples, that it was utterly impossible to acknowledge them personally, nor can I deal with them here. From all over the country I received letters about people in local firms—not millionaires, but executives, managers, directors, people receiving good salaries, people in responsible positions, who have risen from the lowest rung of the ladder, entirely by their own efforts. I especially said that I did not particularly want stories about millionaires, because the number of people who could make a million dollars by their own efforts will always be too small to be important, and because a man of such outstanding ability could probably take care of himself anywhere. And also millionaires, as a class, are not happier than any other type of people. Neither did I want any of the standard "log-cabin-to-White-House" stories of former days which we all know so well. What I wanted was authentic examples of men and women of today who have risen by their own efforts to a responsible position of interesting and well paid work. Such cases would be really significant. Well, as I have said, I got so many that I cannot possibly reproduce them here, and, in any case, I much prefer that the reader should prove it for himself. This you can easily do, and I strongly urge you to do so without delay.

No matter what corner of the United States you may live in you can prove this statement for yourself, right there in your own community within the next few days. Take no one's word, but make a few inquiries at first hand. Try two or three of the principal local factories, and you will find that several, if not most, of the really important positions are held by men who started years ago with no money, no friends, no social influence, and probably at first no education. Find out the stories of your own state and federal congressmen. The governor of the state himself is just as likely, or perhaps even more likely than' not, to have made his own way in life. Inquire about the editors and the chief proprietors of your local newspapers. Select what you consider the best stories in your town or village, and see what the story behind them is. Inquire about the heads of whatever schools and colleges you may have in your district; and do not overlook the public library, the museum, the electric and gas power undertakings, the nearest radio station, or any other human activities that may be going on. With a little practical research of this kind, I claim that you will abundantly prove at first hand that what I say is true, and because these are local examples discovered by yourself, they will be a great deal more convincing than any second-hand examples that I could give you. This condition of things does not even begin to exist in any country outside of the United States.

Again, this country is almost completely free from most of the stupid prejudices that silently poison the very springs of life in other places. In every part of the old world people are steeped and saturated with prejudices of every kind which the young countries have either forgotten or never heard of. They do not mean to be prejudiced. They are not aware of it. These things begin with life itself, are imbibed with the first drops of the mother's milk, and continue to seep in through the pores of the skin, as it were, every day of their lives. Indeed, it is the malice of such prejudice that the victim hardly ever suspects it. People from Europe who settle in America and go home from time to time on visits realize more and more on each occasion this fact of the absence of all kinds of stupid prejudices in the new world. Even the people they admire most in the old countries are apt to seem a little narrow-minded, a little snobbish, a little too satisfied with things as they are. It is difficult to put one's finger on the exact spot, to locate it definitely in words, but beyond any question it is there. It seems to me that a good way to sum up the fundamental difference in outlook between Europe and America is to say that when a new idea or a new method presents itself, Europe says, "Why?" but America says, "Why not?"

Now I have said that I think that most Americans, and especially perhaps the younger generation, tend to take these things—this freedom of opportunity—too much for granted. I want to try to make you realize that they are not just a matter of chance, nor did they spring out of the ground overnight; neither did they fall from heaven complete. In order to exist, this condition of life had to be produced by *people who wanted it*. The people of the generation which produced it, the people of the Revolution, had to think it out. *They had to work for it.* They had to make sacrifices for it. They had to fight for it, and in many cases they had to lay down their lives for it. It did not come easily. The inspiration was there, but, as with every inspiration, it had to be brought out into practical expression; and that is always difficult. It is always easy to copy an older thing with slight alterations, but very difficult to do something really new and really better. In this case the inspiration came to the leaders, to the Fathers of the Constitution, as we call them; but they could have done nothing alone if the people had not responded, and worked, and fought, to make it secure. That generation did its work, made a magnificent success of it, and passed on. But I want you to realize that one generation cannot do any work once and for all.

Each generation really has to do it anew for itself—or it could lose it. Just as this freedom had to be built up by those who wanted it, so it could be lost again through carelessness or indifference. There is no guarantee that any nation is going to have rights and liberties for all time, unless it has the mentality and the courage and the understanding to claim them for all time. One of the truest things ever said is that *the price of liberty is eternal vigilance.*

Unless we are just as determined as were our forefathers to keep freedom and harmony and unity in the nation, we can lose them; just as any man can lose his prosperity, or his health, or his character, if he ceases to value these things and to work for them. Freedom is a thing that must be won anew by each generation for itself.

If you will not take the trouble to serve your country to the small extent of registering and voting at every election, of giving reasonable time to the study of public questions, and of raising your voice in the right way in favor of what you believe to be right and against what you think is wrong, you are betraying your country and helping to make it possible for her to lose her freedom. Our fathers risked all to obtain these rights, and we are only called upon to do a little thinking and a little voting to keep them; and yet even that is too much for some people.

Now let us consider the Constitution itself in a little more detail. In studying it carefully you will find one general principle running right through it, one general spirit underlying every paragraph and every clause; namely, the idea of producing a balance of power, the idea that no one man, and no particular group of people, could seize upon power and dominate everyone else. This was done because the framers of the Constitution well knew that no human being is ever fit to have absolute power over his fellowmen.

The Fathers of the Constitution—Washington, Jefferson, Hamilton, Madison, Monroe, Benjamin Franklin, and the others—were men who knew their subject thoroughly because they had studied it profoundly. They were not just a group of casual people who started a casual thing in a casual way. They had studied the ancient civilizations and the methods of government employed therein. They had studied the medieval systems, and they had studied the various constitutions in force in Europe in their own day. They were well acquainted with the great classical writings on the subject of government, such as those of Plato[3] and Aristotle,[4] as well as the works of later writers like Machiavelli[5] and Sir Thomas More,[6] and with the later European speculations on the subject of Thomas Hobbes,[7] John Locke,[8] Montesquieu,[9] and others. They therefore came to their great task very thoroughly equipped. They knew the results of most of the experiments that had already been made in the world.

Above all, they knew, although perhaps they did not in every case fully realize it, that man is here on earth to develop his soul, to become self-reliant, self-expressive, and self-determined, in order, as we say, to glorify God. This great truth was obtained inspirationally, through

3. *The Republic.*
4. *Politics.*
5. *The Prince.*
6. *Utopia.*
7. *Leviathan, etc.*
8. *On Civil Government.*
9. *Spirit of Laws.*

the same divine inspiration that produced the Great Seal and made the design of the American money what it is.[10]

So they carefully framed the Constitution so that it would prevent any repetition in America of the sort of tyranny which has come about in Europe so many times in the last three thousand years.

For tyranny is nothing new. It has established itself both in Europe and in Asia again and again through the centuries. If Washington and Jefferson could come back today and read the front pages of our newspapers containing the news from Europe, they would find nothing there that they had not already read many times concerning other civilizations. So they were determined to draw up a document in which there should be such a *balance of power* that personal or group tyranny would be impossible. Absolute power would corrupt an archangel— and they knew it. If an archangel should today obtain absolute power over any group of human beings, it would not be very long before he became an arch demon. The fathers of the republic knew that absolute power is always abused, so they balanced the Constitution with a perfect system of checks and safeguards.

It is a remarkable fact that the principles embodied will be found to apply equally well to the government of any lesser organization, and even to the management of the human soul itself. If you wish to develop your personality in an all-round and harmonious way, physically, mentally, and spiritually, you will find that by balancing the faculties of your soul and the various needs of your nature on these principles, you will attain the quickest and surest results in progress. The *spirit* underlying the Constitution, the spirit of a balance of power to permit

10. See chapter 17, "The Historical Destiny of the United States."

freedom of growth, is one of almost universal application.

The American Constitution makes certain assumptions about the average man. It assumes that the average man is a sensible sort of fellow. It assumes that he is honest, and it assumes that he is good-natured. You say, "Well, of course, that is natural." Once more I tell you it is not a matter of course. All the previous civilizations were based on exactly the opposite assumptions. All the polities of the ancient world, and of the Middle Ages in particular, were founded on the idea that the average man is naturally foolish; and that unless he is watched and controlled and regimented and scared half out of his wits, he will get into mischief and damage himself or other people in some way. They assumed that he is dishonest. They assumed that he is extremely selfish, and is usually actuated by the lowest motives. Of course, these statements were never written down anywhere. Statesmen do not write such things—such things do not look well in writing. But they wrote other things down, in technical and diplomatic language, that were based on exactly the premises that I have stated. Only in this Constitution is it assumed that the average man is to be trusted. Now it is easy to see why the Constitution calls definitely for *personal initiative, personal self reliance, personal common sense,* and a disposition to compromise sensibly where there cannot be complete agreement; and why it cannot work without these things.

The story of the drawing up of the Constitution is a most interesting example of what may be called intelligent compromise, without which no large number of free people can live together. Those were very grave days. A terrible war had just been successfully terminated. There was no United States then. There were thirteen independent states with, in some cases, seemingly conflicting interests, conflicting temperaments, and a certain amount of the sheer prejudice, which is never entirely absent from human nature. But these men got together and said in effect: "We cannot all agree on everything; if we insist on trying to do that, the whole thing will fall apart; and, having won the war, we shall lose the peace; so we must be prepared for reasonable give and take if we are to survive as a whole." They did compromise. One state gave up one thing, another state another thing, and the Constitution was the outcome of it.

The American Constitution, then, would be unworkable unless the people were self-reliant, self-determined, and resourceful. There are nations who do not care for these things and do not possess them. I suppose we all have our favorite virtues. My own are self-reliance, initiative, resourcefulness, courage. I like these things better than anything else; but there are people who do not, and there are nations which do not. There are nations, for example, whose people like to be directed and ordered about, who like to be led everywhere and told what to do, and where and when to do it. Such people can do great things in the world through mass action, but they could not work with such a constitution as ours. This Constitution calls for people who prefer to take care of themselves. It is intended for the kind of men and women who desire to manage their own lives, and take their own risks, and fend for themselves, and be personally independent—and these very things are just the outstanding characteristics of the majority of American people.

But notice that, among other things, this policy means that there is sure to be a certain amount of suffering, because, when we are free we always make some mistakes.

A convict in prison has very little chance to make mistakes. He is told when to get up, and when to go to bed, is given his food and obliged to eat it. He is told what clothes to wear, what work to do, and how he is to do it. He is taken out into a yard for exercise, and when it is thought he has had enough exercise he is taken back. He can hardly go wrong, he can hardly make a mistake, but neither, of course, does he ever learn anything. A free man will make mistakes, and he will learn by them. He will suffer, but suffering is worth while when you learn something. When you are not free you cannot learn, and so the suffering is only wasted.

Note very particularly that the Constitution does not guarantee equality of lot. You cannot have equality of lot, because human nature varies. No two men have the same character. No two men have quite the same amount of ability. Again, some will have less talent but a strong character, and go to the top for that reason. Other men— we all know some of them—have great talents, but character is lacking, so they remain at the bottom. This being so, there cannot be equality of lot, but there can be, and there is in America, true equality, which is *equality of opportunity*.

Stupid people sometimes say that the American Spirit is an absurd ideal because men are essentially unequal. The local electrician, they point out, is not the equal of Edison; and Emerson was not the equal of the man who groomed his horse. Of course, the authors of the Constitution were perfectly aware of this fact, and it is precisely this fact which they had in mind when the Constitution was designed by them. In a free country, equality means equality of opportunity to make the most of one's talents; and equality before the law, which must not discriminate between one citizen and another. It means the absence of special privilege of any kind, under any pretense.

The Declaration of Independence does not say that men are *born* free and equal, because they are not so born. It says "*created* equal"—quite a different thing. Of course, we are all born different. It is equality of opportunity that matters, and it is equality of opportunity that the Constitution sets out to produce. Now we see that in this way, in this seemingly rather dry legal document, these inspired men were producing a general model for human government. Sooner or later the rest of the world will adopt the principles of the American Constitution. Human nature, being what it is, each people or nation will probably call it its own constitution, but it will be essentially the American Constitution, and it does not matter at all what they call it as long as they put it into effect.

The world today is relatively much smaller than it used to be owing to improved means of transit and communication. The automobile, the airplane, the telegraph, and the radio have made the dangers of over-centralization much greater than they were in the days of Washington, when it was a ten day journey for the average man from the Potomac to New York.

For this reason it is apparent now that the only practical alternatives to the principles of the Constitution are either a *military* despotism—call it what you will—administered by soldiers; or a *bureaucratic* despotism of permanent civil servants, whether you call it socialism or communism. Both of these systems undertake to guarantee to supply the individual with the physical necessaries, and both equally deny him the mental and spiritual bread of life. For this reason they are both eternally unacceptable to those who possess the American Spirit, quite apart from the fact that with any kind of despotic government, the grossest corruption is certain to creep in sooner or later because criticism is not allowed. So, if you do not wish to become the serf either of swashbuckling military adventurers, on the one hand, or of a soulless impersonal bureaucracy on the other, you must take a definite stand for personal freedom and the principles of the Constitution. You must care enough about it to defend it vigorously in every way that you can.

The Constitution is not an experiment. I was amazed the other day to hear an American (and supposedly a cultured one) say, with a shake of his head, "It is a remarkable experiment." An experiment after a century and a half! That is not a bad run for an experiment, an experiment which now includes over 130,000,000 people on a subcontinent containing every kind of climate and almost every kind of natural condition. So far from being an experiment, the Constitution has justified itself completely. It has been an unqualified success. Any real difficulty that this country has had will be found upon analysis always to have originated in some departure from the spirit, if not of the letter, of the Constitution. Think it over for yourself. Read the history of the country, and you will find that the difficulties and embarrassments which the United States has had to meet in the last one hundred and fifty years and more, have always resulted from a departure from the spirit of the Constitution.

The Constitution has amply justified itself. It has given the people the highest standard of living in the world. The poorest people in the United States are still better off than the poor in any other country. In spite of eight or nine years of depression panic—and it is only a panic of fear—in spite of other difficulties, there is still a higher standard of living in this country than in any other. And the next highest standard, note carefully, is in the other free countries. It is in the countries where freedom and the rights of the individual have been trampled underfoot that the lowest general standard of living prevails.

The Constitution has produced the highest standard of living. It has produced the greatest educational opportunities. There are more opportunities for education in this country, particularly for the poor boy or girl, than in any place in the world. There are more chances for success and self-realization, and for prosperity and happiness for the average man in this country than anywhere else.

Under the Constitution, the country has prospered materially. It has won every war into which it has entered. And in general, the history of its dealings with other countries has been highly creditable. Never allow people from other countries to deceive or bamboozle you into the idea that the United States makes more mistakes than other nations, because it is not true. The United States has made mistakes, of course, because it is made up of human beings, and for the same reason will probably make more in the future, but all the other nations have made their mistakes too and without exception they have made many more and worse mistakes than we have. Here is the difference: This being a young country, and a free and democratic country, all the mistakes and errors are dragged out into the open and exposed, whereas in other countries, mistakes are hushed up, and a false front of propriety is shown to the world. Even in the countries where there is a free press, the tendency is to put as good a face as possible upon everything, so as not to give the country a "black eye." The feeling is that the press is the nation's shop window, and should therefore be dressed as becomingly as possible. In America, however, on the other hand, everything is dragged out, and our press seems actually to delight in making everything seem as bad as possible. On the whole, this tendency is a good and healthy one, for it is better to know the worst than to live with a false sense of security.

So, please remember that foreign countries are never nearly as virtuous as they seem; and that in the United States things are always much better than they seem. It has been said that it is a peculiarity of Americans that they will allow a scandal or a mistake to continue rather longer than would be allowed in most other countries; and they then get mad and tear the whole thing down, and clean it up, and put something else there that is far better than anything to be found elsewhere. This is probably true, and there is a thoroughness about it which appeals to me.

One of the criticisms of this country that is often heard is the alleged existence of political corruption, or graft, as the newspapers call it. Now there is undoubtedly some ground for this complaint, but it must be pointed out, first of all, that the amount and extent of political corruption has been grossly exaggerated. Unquestionably it exists; but unquestionably too the overwhelming majority of men in politics—city, state, and federal—are honest and sincere men doing the best they can in the circumstances. On the other hand, there is no foreign country without a good deal of "graft" too. In the older lands, however, the graft is much more scientifically, and, one may say, artistically carried out. There is none of the crudeness that makes it public property in this country. It is concealed in ways that generations of experience have made practicable, but nevertheless it exists, and it requires very little knowledge of human nature to realize that the more despotic the institutions of a country are, the more the hidden graft will flourish.

The reason political corruption exists at all in America is this. In this new and immense nation there are so many interesting and worthwhile things to do in the general development of the country that the best type of minds have no incentive to go into politics. Politicians, therefore, have tended to be of an inferior grade of ability and character. During the wonderful development of a new continent it is not natural that the somewhat humdrum business of political administration should attract the best types of men as it does in old countries where there are few other opportunities for a career. Now, however, it is obvious that public opinion has awakened, and that political corruption really is at last on the way out; and I have no doubt that before very long it will be practically a thing of the past in the United States.

Another criticism of which we hear much is the supposed existence of more crime in this country than abroad. A fair consideration, however, indicates that this problem too is being overcome. It must be remembered that the detection and arrest of a criminal is much more difficult here. In France or England or Germany for example, we find a homogeneous population having the same traditions and the same training. These countries too are in mere extent very small, and so it is much more difficult for a wanted criminal to conceal himself in England or in France. The United States is an immense continent, and there is still quite a mixture of races and traditions, and these will naturally tend to facilitate the operations of the crook. Also the existence of forty-eight semi-independent jurisdictions in this country has naturally made it easier for dishonest persons to escape the hand of justice; but this difficulty is now being overcome by the federal authorities.

Let us be clear also that the crime difficulty has not been a permanent thing in the United States, but was really a wave that followed the Great War, and the depression which made it impossible for young men to find work. When you take into account also the complete failure of the prohibition experiment, for which public opinion was quite unready, and the premium which it placed on law breaking of many kinds, it will be seen that the unfortunate outburst of crime which has marked recent years is really an exceptional and a passing thing.

Perhaps it will not be out of order to point out that the most serious crimes have usually been committed, not by Americans, but by foreign immigrants or their children, who had not yet had time to absorb the American Spirit. In many cases these desperadoes came from countries in which there had been no freedom and no secure government since the Roman Empire, and where the people, therefore, had never been educated to respect or to trust the law. Here again it is obvious that it is only a question of time before these evils automatically remedy themselves.

The United States has nothing to fear in the future as long as her people remain united in thought and feeling, and this they are certain to do. Two Americans, from no matter what different parts of the country they may come, or what the difference in their circumstances may be, will always have much more in common between them than either can possibly have in common with any foreigner, and this fundamental fact must be paramount in its influence.

So the Constitution gives us the foundation for a free, prosperous, and independent life for every citizen. The old fashioned phrase, "plain Jeffersonian democracy," expresses the essential idea of the Constitution very well—as does the White House itself. A visit to the White House is a moral and spiritual tonic. Its simple, quiet dignity makes Versailles and Potsdam and such places seem almost theatrical and tawdry in comparison. It is not a palace, but the residence of a private gentleman who is acting as Chief Magistrate of the Nation for the time being. Most of the Presidents of the last hundred and fifty years have exemplified the same idea in their personal lives. Both Washington and Lincoln perfectly expressed that idea in their very different ways. Calvin Coolidge,[11] when the news of his succession reached him, happened to be staying in the humble farmhouse of his father; that father was a magistrate, and the new President was sworn into office there and then on the family Bible. I have been told that Theodore Roosevelt was sworn in by a neighbor in much the same way; and it is certain that when the family moved to Washington his younger children were promptly sent to the nearest public school. Sentimentalities? I think not. They seem to me to be merely practical examples of the general outlook which we have been considering.

A true American will take pains to incorporate that outlook in every phase of his life. If he happens to be rich, he will carefully avoid all senseless luxury and unnecessary display; or anything which may tend to set artificial barriers between himself and his fellow citizens. If he happens not to be rich, he will not allow any false

11. As Vice President he assumed the Presidency on the death of the President.

ideals to give him a sense of inferiority on that account, for he will understand that it is character that really matters.

Such, in broad outline, is the spirit of the American Constitution, and I, for one, am proud to pay my personal tribute to the lofty vision and the practical statesmanship it embodies.

The Historical
Destiny of the United States

The Mystery of the American Money

I N order to understand the special work which the United States has been called upon to do in the history of Humanity, we have first to remember that the American people are, historically, that section of the people of Europe whose task it was to explore the continent of America, to subdue it, and to develop it.

It is impossible to understand the historical significance and importance of any country as long as we consider that country only by itself. In order to determine its true place in the scheme of things, we have to consider its connection with the general stream of historical tendencies. It is needless to say that a purely partisan outlook—the so-called "patriotic" outlook, for instance—is a hopeless handicap to the finding of the truth. In the study of history as in the investigations of natural science, the truth is arrived at only after an impartial and dispassionate inquiry.

Now, the historical background out of which the United States arose was really the old Feudal civilization of Europe. All modern history grows out of the Roman Empire; all our reckonings go back to that as a kind of datum line. The ancient civilizations culminated in the Roman Empire, and the medieval and modern cultures and polities grew out of it. The Roman Empire gradually broke up and disappeared owing to various causes with which I am not at present concerned; it was followed by the chaotic condition that we call the Dark Ages; and then, gradually, quite without the conscious knowledge or intention of those concerned, the great Feudal civilization came into being. That Medieval Feudal civilization was a wonderful attainment, and for hundreds of years it provided the European Race with exactly the social and political instrument that it needed for its growth and self-expression. It furnished a body of traditions, customs, laws, and institutions, by no means perfect—no human arrangement ever is—but on the whole useful and adequate for the work that had to be done.

All good things, however, outgrow their usefulness and come to an end, and as man's expanding knowledge and the expanding power that grows from expanding knowledge accumulated, the Feudal System gradually grew out of date, as the Roman Empire had done before it, and the imperative need arose for a new and a much wider and freer state of society. Such great changes seldom come easily. The outworn thing seldom abdicates the remnants of its decaying authority without a struggle, and so Feudalism died hard and long, not succumbing finally until the end of the First World War. The great spiritual and intellectual movements that we call the Renaissance, the Reformation, the Industrial Revolution, the French Revolution, and especially, as I intend to show, the Revolution of the American Colonists, were all single acts in this one great drama.

The closing of the direct route to the East led to the discovery of America by Columbus in 1492, and this gave a tremendous impetus to men's imaginations. The invention of a practicable printing press liberated their minds and made the Reformation, which, in principle, meant the repudiation of authority in spiritual matters, inevitable; and this point once gained, political freedom could only be a matter of time and opportunity. The only question was where and how it would come about.

In spite of the revolutionary changes which had been accomplished in mental and spiritual things, Feudalism, on its political and social side, was still strongly entrenched as late as the middle of the eighteenth century. In spite of the Reformation, in spite of the Utopian dreams of certain book-men and philosophers, there was nothing like political freedom, as we understand it today, anywhere in Europe. Relatively a little more free in some places, relatively a little less free in others, the hard fact was that men were afraid (however they might think) to say or do whatever they liked, as long as what they liked might be unwelcome to the powers in authority.

But when once any degree of spiritual freedom has been won, by an individual, or by a nation, it is then but a question of time before that inner freedom expresses itself in the outer; and so it was inevitable that humanity should achieve political freedom too; and the only question was where the thing should begin. The only question was in which country occupied by the White Race the seed of liberty should come to fruition. When we think of the map of Europe in the mid-eighteenth century from north to south and from east to west, we seek in vain for a likely place where this might happen. Everywhere, of course, there were individuals who were quite ready for the new thing, but nowhere was there a steady current of public opinion in its favor, much less an established government likely to tolerate anything of the kind.

It is only when we turn our gaze from Europe and look across the North Atlantic Ocean to the new or still comparatively new colonies of European people on the Eastern seaboard of America that we find something like what we are seeking. Here at least we have, not by any means perhaps the ideal democracy dreamed of by the poets, but at least a relatively simple, and, compared with Europe, an exceedingly democratic community in which the realities of Feudalism had never been able to take root, because the heart of Feudalism itself was dead before these colonies began. In the New World even the strongest Tory, in name, was such a long way from home and from the natural atmosphere of Feudalism, that without knowing it he was, in many things that mattered, a good deal more radical than most of the Whigs in London.

Some of the most influential communities in America had been founded and built up by religious refugees fleeing from persecution at home; and so, even in the presence of Blue Laws and not a little Puritanical tyranny, the main subconscious stream of thought and feeling—the thing that really sways public opinion—was definitely without any of those deep instincts of unquestioning respect for established authority that was still so much a part of the mind of Europe.

We see, therefore, that it was entirely natural when the time had come for the European White Race to cast off the shackles of Feudalism and begin to establish political freedom, that the great spiritual urge, for such it was, should take the line of least resistance and come forth, not in France, not in England, not in Germany, but in what were then called the American Colonies. In other words, the American Revolution was no mere brawl between England, the Mother Land, and a rebellious colony, which might perhaps have been averted by a more clever diplomacy, or a quicker use of force, or the hazard of a battle or so. It was nothing less than a part, and a vital part, of the great march of Humanity on the road to freedom. For, let there be no mistake, the march of Humanity, despite what the short-sighted pessimists may say, is ever onward and upward toward greater, and finer, and better things. Temporary set-backs there may be from time to time in this country or that, but the general sweep of history is forward and upward toward freedom.

It was inevitable that the movement for effective democratic government should break out among that body of people which had staked all for the right to seek spiritual truth wherever it might lead them, and the right to worship God in their own way.

And so the Colonies revolted; fought a terrific battle; won it; and established—at any rate in principle—the doctrine that just governments derive their authority from the consent of the governed, and not from any supposed Divine right, or any right of conquest or brute force. For our purpose there is no need to consider the details of the struggle, or to assess the worth or otherwise of the personalities concerned therein. The folly of King George the Third and the stupidity of General Burgoyne on one side, and the unique character of George Washington on the other side, are independent of the principle involved. That the Colonies would have won when they did without the extraordinary combination of qualities possessed by Washington is unlikely; but had they not won then they would have done so later on, because an independent United States was inevitable. This country had to be independent of any European government in order to fulfill her historical destiny.

The essential point that we have to note is that, in the principles which they proclaimed in the Declaration of Independence and other documents, the Fathers of the Constitution definitely set the headline and the example which was afterward followed by the Heralds of Freedom everywhere. They set the standards with their brains and hearts, and by their military success they made them possible as an accomplished fact.

Thus the successful revolution of the American Colonists was no mere local victory for the Thirteen Colonies. It was nothing less than one of the great turning points in the history of Humanity, because it definitely diverted the main stream of history in a particular direction. In setting the pattern for the later development of the European race, it set the ultimate pattern for all humanity. Had not a democratic republic been set up on the American continent in 1776, the French Revolution, which followed thirteen years later, would not have taken the course that it did; and had not the French Revolution taken the course that it did, the whole history of the world, not only today but for all future ages, must have been different too.

It was the success of the American Revolution that established the doctrine of the Rights of Man in its true sense, as the doctrine of the right to individual freedom on all planes which belongs to man as the image and likeness of God; for that is what the phrase in the Declaration of Independence concerning life, liberty, and the pursuit of happiness really means. This assertion of the Divine Right of every man and woman to develop in his own way is the fundamental Right of Man; and although, largely in consequence of the chaos arising out of the World War, that principle may temporarily be lost sight of in certain places, yet, the eclipse is but temporary, and in the long run the victory of freedom will be won.

The French Revolution, influenced much more than many people realize by what had happened in America, took its course, and the French Revolution has been echoing through the history of the world ever since. The work it did for human freedom was so fundamental and sweeping that—because of its very success—we sometimes tend to underrate its importance today. Because the old Feudal world that it swept away has so utterly gone that we have to go to the old Czarist Russia to find anything like it, we can easily forget how bad it became, and what an appalling thing this Feudalism in its decay and slow death could be. The French Revolution, however, has marched up and down the world in the last one hundred and forty years (it reached Spain only the other day), and all that wave of freedom sprang in essentials from the lead given by the American Colonists in their successful establishing of the United States.

The English-speaking peoples have always been pioneers in the cause of human freedom. They have always felt intuitively that personal freedom is the first and greatest good, and that no other boon could possibly compensate for the loss of that. In the Old World and in the New they have led Humanity in the establishment of personal liberty, and in the science and art of self-government, which is its only guarantee. It was the English people in the Old World who struck the first blow for individual freedom. All through their history they challenged the idea of despotic rule in either politics or religion, and whenever their conditions were not so difficult as to make it impossible, they established liberty,

as far as might be, in fact. The *Magna Charta,* the Habeas
Corpus Act, the Bill of Rights, effective trial by jury, were
all England's gift to the world. She got angry and cut off
one king's head, in pursuit of this principle; and there is
no saying what she might not have done to another king,
if he had not run away out of the country before he could
be caught. Parliamentary institutions in their effective
form had their origin, of course, in the "Mother of Par-
liaments"; and the American Colonists in their revolt
against the British Crown were but acting in perfect con-
formity with the old English traditions.

There is no doubt that if the majority of the English
people could have been consulted in 1776, their verdict
would have been in favor of the Colonists. George Washington had to fight for his life, not against the English
people, but against the small close Oligarchy which held
them in its power.

The people of England had no effective voice in the
election of governments, and therefore in controlling
their policies, until the Reform Act of 1832. Green, the
historian, in his standard work says of this time:

> At a time when it had become all-powerful in the
> State, the House of Commons had ceased in any
> real and effective sense to be a representative
> body at all. . . . Great towns like Manchester or
> Birmingham remained without a member, while
> members still sat for boroughs which, like Old
> Sarum, had actually vanished from the face of the
> earth. . . . Even in towns which had a real claim to
> representation, the narrowing of municipal privi-
> leges . . . to a small part of the inhabitants and in
> many cases the restriction of electoral rights to the
> members of the governing corporation, rendered

their representation a mere name. . . . *Out of a population of eight millions, only one hundred and sixty thousand were electors at all.* How far such a House was from really representing English opinion we see from the fact that in the height of his popularity Pitt could hardly find a seat in it . . . a reformer could allege without a chance of denial, "This House is not a representative of the people of Great Britain. It is the representative of nominal boroughs, of ruined and exterminated towns, of noble families, of wealthy individuals, of foreign potentates." . . . The Parliament indeed had become supreme, and in theory the Parliament was a representative of the whole English people. But in actual fact, the bulk of the English people found itself powerless to control the course of English government.

The British Overseas Empire, too, may be said to owe its freedom to the American victory. It was the lesson of Yorktown, thoroughly learned and digested by the English governing caste, that led to the grant of complete self-government to the British Dominions, one after another, without which they would not have remained under the British flag for a generation. As it is, those Dominions now enjoy complete freedom, and are virtually independent republics. They are loyal and satisfied members of the British Commonwealth of Nations because of their freedom, and not in despite of it. This Commonwealth is not a federal system, but a chain of free alliances. It is, among other things, a splendid guarantee against war between any of these countries.

Having now traced the development of intellectual, social, and political freedom, we come to the next step of capital importance in the history of Humanity, and that is the coming forth of the new ideas that we call Truth, or Divine Science. This great revelation is really primitive Christianity, or the doctrine of the Allness and Availability of God. It is the doctrine that God is everywhere present, at all times, and that every man and woman has the right and the power of direct access to God, without the mediation of any person, or institution, or other human authority, and it is the real meaning of the clause in the Declaration of Independence which says: "All men are created equal." This was the next great step forward for Humanity, and here again the question arises: Where should, where could, such a doctrine appear with any prospect of being received by the people?

Let us pause here for a moment to consider what this teaching means. The doctrine of the Allness and the immediate Availability of God is, beyond any question, the most revolutionary as well as the most important discovery that the human race has ever made. The Immanence of God in His creation has always been known to the more advanced members of the race, but only the very few have ever understood what is for us the most vital implication of that doctrine, namely, that the Immanence of God means that God is instantly available to any human being who will turn to Him in thought for healing, for inspiration, for help of any kind. The discovery of this fact is easily the most important event that ever happened for either the race or the individual. What is there that could compare with it for a single moment? When you consider the terrible struggle that the human race has had to reach even our present comparatively backward condition—for as long as sickness, poverty, and, above all, war, continue, how can we call ourselves anything but backward—when you consider the terrific struggle that most men and women of all races and in all ages have had to obtain even the amount of health, prosperity, and happiness that they do possess, you will realize what a transcendent discovery is this knowledge that the power of God, Infinite Power, and Intelligence, and Love, can be brought to bear upon every one of our problems and that we no longer have to depend upon our own feeble and flickering efforts.

This is really scientific Christianity—the original Christian message. It is found all through the Bible, but it is not until we reach the New Testament that it is explicitly stated. Unhappily, the Christian movement was allowed to become a Department of State under Constantine, whereupon the Spiritual Idea rapidly faded out of men's minds. From time to time as the centuries went on the original message of Jesus was partially rediscovered by various spiritually minded people; in particular George Fox, the founder of the Quakers, got very near to it indeed; but it was not until about the second quarter of the nineteenth century that the Spiritual Idea again emerged in its fullness.

Several things, we now see, had to happen before the great modern Renaissance of the Truth could take place. The first thing was the intellectual preparation. The Spiritual Idea is a purely spiritual experience; but to be intelligently applied it needs also to be apprehended by the intellect. Unless you have some intellectual understanding of the theory underlying it, you will be able to apply it only occasionally and by chance. There are, of course, many people who have it only in that way today. They get results from time to time, by the exercise of the feeling nature alone, not having any clear understanding of what they are doing; but this means that one is never really master of the Word, as we are entitled to be.

The majority of students of Truth, however, now fully appreciate the need for some intellectual apprehension in order to complete their spiritual understanding, and it is this fact that is our guarantee that the Truth will not be lost again as it was about the fourth century.

In order that people should have such an intellectual apprehension it is necessary for them to have the concept of Natural Law. Probably the greatest fundamental difference between what we call modern times and the rest of history is that, for the first time in the evolution of the race, the general public understands the idea of Natural Law. Today even school children realize thoroughly that they live in a world that is governed by law, and not by chance. They quite understand that if the electric light fails it is because the laws of electricity have been broken at some point in the circuit—a fuse blown, a lamp burned out, or a defective switch. It never occurs to them that the putting out of the light is an arbitrary action of God in order to punish someone. Again, when an epidemic attacks a town, people understand that some mistake has been made somewhere, usually the mistake we call dirt; whereas in former times it was assumed as a matter of course that plague came to the city as a direct act of God, and without reference to sanitary or any other conditions. In the same way, good and bad harvests, the striking of a building by lightning, earthquakes, tidal waves, and all other natural phenomena are now perfectly well understood as following natural laws. In other words, no one supposes that God manifests His majesty by breaking the Laws of Being, but rather by fulfilling them.

Now this conception of Natural Law simply had to be generally accepted by the public at large before the teaching that we call Truth could become widespread among the people. The whole idea of spiritual treatment or Scientific Prayer is the reliance upon the fact of God as Principle. Our reliance, which is the secret of all spiritual demonstration, is upon the fact that God, who is Infinite Harmony, cannot either cause or endorse anything but perfect harmony in His manifestation.

In all ages people have said their prayers in the spirit of asking God to perform a special miracle on their behalf, there and then, suspending natural laws "just this once" in order to get them out of a fix. But in order that spiritual truth should prevail, and prayer become really scientific, man had to reach the stage where the appeal to God to help him was not for a breach of natural laws, but rather that the power of God should *fulfill* the law of harmony to get him out of his trouble. Such an attitude could not have been generally obtained much before the nineteenth century. Here in the twentieth century and henceforth forever, it is the only attitude that the people will ever consent to adopt. People brought up in the orthodox way of thought have in so many cases given up prayer altogether just because they had reached that stage of intellectual unfoldment where they could not bring themselves to ask for a private miracle without feeling ridiculous. The understanding of the Allness of God teaches us that it is sin, sickness, and death that are our own "private miracles," and that all-round harmony and happiness is the standard condition of life as designed by God.

The intellectual understanding of law was one of the conditions needed for the re-birth of this truth; and an outward condition of political freedom with a tradition of personal independence of judgment was the other essential factor.

We will now pause to consider why, when this doctrine was to come into the world, it should need the special social and political conditions which were only to be found in the United States, and to provide which, in fact, the United States had really been brought into existence. It actually came into expression among the simple, unlearned, everyday people of New England—farmers, small traders, artisans, and so forth. A great idea never arrives in the world at one isolated point: it always "comes through" at about the same time, but in varied degrees of clearness, in a number of different places. When we understand that there is a general race-mind common to all human beings, we see why this must be so. These ideas percolate through at various points whenever, for one reason or another, there is an easy passage. We say that certain ideas are "in the air." Now these ideas were "in the air," i.e., in the race-mind, at this period; and so it happened that several people got them in various degrees of intensity about the same time. There has since been some little discussion in various quarters as to who should have the honor of priority, but that point is of no importance whatever. The honor of priority, if it is to go to anyone, probably belongs to Phineas Park Quimby, a practical clockmaker of Portland, Maine. Quimby was quite without what is conventionally called education. He had practically no schooling, much less scholarship; but he was naturally a very spiritual man, and he had the great quality of open-mindedness, and much natural intelligence. Like Faraday, a working bookbinder and a genius of somewhat similar type who is sometimes called the Father of Electrical Engineering, Quimby had a natural gift for scientific experimentation, and this he applied to the subject of mental and spiritual healing. But the thing was in the air generally. Emerson, of course, is the prophet of the teaching—but Emerson with his academic detachment from actualities did not discover its practical application to the healing of the body and affairs. Prentice Mulford got it too, independently, but by no means as clearly as Quimby did, and he seems never to have distinguished definitely between the spiritual and the psychic. There were a number of other pioneers too.

A natural question that presents itself at this point is this: Why was this discovery, the most important discovery in the whole history of mankind, left to a self-educated working clockmaker? Why was the discovery not made at Harvard, or Yale, or Oxford, or Cambridge, or any of the great centers of learning on the Continent? Why, for that matter, was not the Great Truth revealed to one of the Bishops or Archbishops, or to any of the recognized intellectual or spiritual leaders? Is it that the Holy Spirit has a preference for simple uneducated people, and a prejudice against learning and leadership? The answer is, of course, that the Holy Spirit, which really means the Wisdom of God in action, has no preferences whatever. Do we not know that God is no respecter of persons? But there is one indispensable condition that must be present if spiritual revelation is to be received— there must be an open mind, and freedom from spiritual pride. Jesus formulated this rule when he said, "If you want to enter the Kingdom of Heaven you must become like a little child," and our modern academic education, both religious and secular, has manifested one paralyzing defect—it has not developed spiritual or intellectual humility. On the contrary, it has displayed a fatal tendency to foster spiritual pride. Men and women of academic training too often come to feel—not always consciously—that things must happen in a certain way, because that is the way that they have been trained to expect them to happen—and the voice of God is forever whispering "Behold, I make all things new."

Other things being equal, this message would have come to the leaders of the great universities, or to the heads of the great churches, because, in consequence of their official positions, such people would have been able to give the message out more quickly, and to larger numbers of people than any obscure man could have done; and as Divine Wisdom always chooses the way of efficiency it would have chosen such channels in preference; but alas, these channels were closed. The clearest open channel for the Jesus Christ teaching was the clockmaker of Portland, and because we always get at all times just what we deserve (which means just what we are ready for), the clockmaker got the revelation. Once more the finger of God had put down the mighty from their seats, and exalted the humble and unknown.

Granted that the Great Message had to come through an humble channel, why could it not have happened in any country in Europe? Why were conditions to be found only in America so necessary? The answer is that in Europe, still lying under the declining shadow of the Feudal Age, many an humble soul was indeed a clear enough channel for the reception of the Truth; but, though such a one might receive the idea of the Truth, he was not likely to have sufficient faith in his own judgment to accept the inspiration that he received; nor, if he did, would it have been possible, with the social and political conditions prevailing, for him to have put it out.

Let us suppose that a clockmaker or a peasant in England had received this great idea. He would almost certainly have consulted the rector of his parish or the minister of his chapel about the wonderful thing that had come to him. That rector or minister might have received him with kindness but would certainly have said: "These ideas of yours look attractive and sound very well, but they cannot be true because they do not agree with the teaching of our church. Therefore they are false and pernicious, and the very fact that they are naturally attractive makes them all the more dangerous to those who have the misfortune to contact them. Say no more about this to anyone, and endeavor to forget it yourself. Satan, who is ever busy, and subtle beyond computation, has laid a snare for you." In Germany or Scandinavia the local pastor, and in France or Italy the parish priest would have received him in almost identically the same way. Only in the United States was there, at that date, a tradition of personal independence among the plain people which could make both the reception and the publication of the Great Message possible. And so it was in the United States that the thing happened.

So now we see that when the time had arrived for Humanity to take its great step, the ground had been prepared by the placing of a selected body of the people of Europe upon a new continent, which was the only way in which they could be set free from the bondage of innumerable outworn traditions and habits of thought. They have been placed upon a new continent because they have a new work to do for the human race. And now we shall consider in a broad way what that work is.

The historical destiny of the United States is first of all the bringing to birth of this Truth, that for convenience we are calling Divine Science, by providing the only atmosphere in which it could be born and live; secondly, the United States is destined to produce a new nation completely different from any of the nations already existing; and, thirdly, she is destined to establish a new order of society as different from Feudalism as Feudalism was from the other civilizations that preceded it. This new order which has gradually been taking shape on this continent, I am going to call for want of a better term, the American Dream. The term has been used a good deal by one or two modern writers, and it will serve my purpose very well; and I am now going to ask you to consider what really is the American Dream.

The American Dream is no passing romantic fantasy, but actually a new attitude to life, and a new order of society. The American Dream stands for, among other things, the idea that all men and women, irrespective of who their parents were, are to have equal rights and opportunities. It is the firm faith that ability of every kind occurs indiscriminately in all classes of the community, and that the poor and friendless child is just as likely, given the opportunity, to develop nobility of character, or intellectual or spiritual talents, as the most highly connected child in the land. It embodies the idea that men and women, when they are not segregated from one another by artificial barriers of social caste, can get along well together, and that mutual service and mutual co-operation flourish best in these conditions. It discourages all artificial distinctions. It says, in effect, "the tools to him who can use them." The American Dream includes the idea that the plain man can and will rise to any occasion when he is thrown upon his own responsibility, and will be equal to any emergency that may arise; and it contains, implicitly, the idea that there is no difficulty that humanity cannot overcome if it really wishes to, because "where there's a will there's a way."

In Europe, and still more in Asia, there has always been a feeling that there are certain ills that must be borne, because they are unconquerable, and there is no way out;

but to the true American Spirit nothing is unconquerable. It delights in tackling difficult problems. The American Spirit sets no store upon the sense of awe, nor has it any exaggerated respect for anything in particular, either alive or dead. Authority of any kind is lightly esteemed, and this is because of the intuitive feeling that our outer conditions really are essentially mutable, and that the individual has dominion over all things. And all this, of course, is fundamentally what we call Divine Science.

For this great work which is to be done upon the American Continent—remember that the American Dream is only beginning to be worked out—for this great work, Divine Providence has selected its instruments with great care. Every nation in the world has a special work to do for the whole race which no other nation can do, just as every individual person has his own work to do that no one else can do; and so the new nation that is now being formed upon this continent is to be quite different from any other nation yet existing. The American Nation is to be as different from the English Nation, or the French Nation, or the German Nation, or the Italian Nation, as these are one from another. But how is a new nation made? Well a new nationality does not appear in history ready-made out of nowhere, as Minerva sprang complete from the brain of Jupiter. There is, of course, no such thing as a "pure-blooded" race or nation. Such a thing would be opposed to the essential principles of biology. History shows that a new nation has always been made by selecting individuals from various older nations, and combining them into something new. As in chemistry a new compound having new and quite novel properties is formed by a fresh grouping of old elements, so a new nation is always built by a re-grouping of individuals from older ones. The great Roman Nation was a new and very wonderful grouping of a number of ancient tribes which had never been grouped in that way before. The great and unique French Nation is a special combination of the Frank and the Gaul and other older nations. The English people are themselves a special amalgam of quite a number of contributing strains. Tennyson says, "Saxon and Norman and Dane are we"—and he might have added, "a lot of Roman soldiers and many Celts, and a miscellaneous crowd of later immigrants too," while he was about it; for all these strains have contributed to form the modern Englishman.

The elements which are to make up the new American Nation have been selected by Providence with great care from every nation in Europe. English, Irish, Scotch, Dutch, Germans, Italians, Scandinavians and others, all have contributed their quota. The Teuton, the Latin, the Slav, as well as the Anglo-Saxon, have been drawn upon, and all because Nature has determined to do something new. Anglo-Saxons might think that a purely Anglo-Saxon selection would have been better; Teutons might think that a pure Germanic nation would have been a far better plan; and undoubtedly many Latins and Slavs would have their own views on the subject too; but Providence knew best. She decided to have something quite new, because she never repeats herself.

Now, how were the people destined to be the builders of the new nation to be selected? In other words, how was it to be determined who should come to America and who should not? Imagine to yourself that Providence had consulted you on this vital point, and ask yourself how you would have collected your immigrants. Well, perhaps if you knew very little of history you would have chosen the most distinguished citizens socially and educationally in the Old World—but history teaches us

that such people, admirable in themselves, do not produce anything new, and that they do not last very long.
When an aristocracy comes to its full flower, then, history tells us, it begins to decay. Or, perhaps you would
have set a number of competitive examinations; and then
you would have got—well, most of us have an idea of what
you would have got. Most of us have an idea of what is
the usual career of the prize boy at school. We seldom
hear of him again as doing anything in particular, certainly not building up a new civilization. Perhaps you
would have tried to set some kind of test, or trap, or net,
for a particular kind of people. That plan has been tried
too. All through history emperors and governments have
tried making artificial plantations of hand-picked people in various territories, and nothing has ever come of
that except, as a rule, a great deal of local friction, and
final disappointment.

The question we have to ask ourselves is, what qualities
we should wish to select. If we rise above the first great
danger of selecting the kind of people who would be likely
to do the kind of things that we happen to approve of,
rather than something new, we shall probably agree that
to build up a new civilization the qualities we should need
are qualities of character, because these are the things
that cannot be taught or imparted by artificial means.
Knowledge, technical training, good manners, and correct
social habits can all be acquired without much difficulty,
at least in a generation or two, if the fundamentals of
character are there to begin with; and the fundamentals
we need are, first of all, courage—physical courage and
moral courage—and spiritual courage too. We need enterprise. We need energy that will not be denied an out-
let. We need perseverance and determination. Above all,

we need self-reliance and resourcefulness. We need a willingness to break with old tradition and a readiness to assume the new outlook.

Now how are people possessing these qualities to be selected from among their neighbors who do not possess them? Well, there is only one way to do it, and that was the way in which Providence arranged that the United States should receive those elements that are to build up her future; namely, by spontaneous emigration. General and spontaneous emigration to a new land of opportunity automatically sifts out, on the whole, just those qualities which we have been enumerating. It is the people who possess essentially such qualities as these who, in the long run, pull up their stakes in an old country and emigrate to a new one; for please remember that emigration is no easy business.

Consider the conditions of life in an old country with a settled and not easily changed order of things. It will probably be overpopulated for its resources, and opportunities will be very restricted for the average man or woman, and for the poor they will hardly exist at all. To follow in his father's footsteps along the same rut will, in most cases, be the highest that the peasant or workman can hope for in any part of Europe. Exceptional individuals will rise up from the bottom to the top, but they will always be very exceptional—white blackbirds. Now all young people, for a season at least, are ambitious and adventurous up to a point—"the thoughts of youth are long, long thoughts." In the evenings in every country in Europe boys and girls will meet together after the day's toil, and talk about the restrictions of their lives, the absence of opportunities, the meagerness of their earnings, the obtuseness of their parents, and such things;

and very often half a dozen of them talking together will agree, "I am tired of this; there is nothing for me here; I will go to America."

Ten years later, twenty years later, out of that half dozen, one will be in America, while all the rest are still grumbling over their restrictions, or else comforting themselves with some kind of self-deception, as people do. Now which of the six will on the average have reached America? Do you not see that it must be just the one who possesses, in the highest degree, the qualities which we have enumerated. To make the great, and for them terribly expensive, journey from the old village street to the New World has, in these simple people, called for qualities which in truth are nothing less than heroic. Thus has America received her human material.

Thus a new nation is being formed, and on a scale and with a rapidity that has never happened before in the history of mankind. Look at the story of this continent during the brief three centuries or so that the American people have been here; look at it with some sense of historical perspective; and ask yourself if any great national work has ever been carried out on such a scale and at such a speed before. A whole continent has been explored and subdued and to a large extent developed in that time, and the political and social ground-plan of a mighty nation has been definitely laid down. Almost all the old precedents and traditions have been successfully broken through, and a new method, and a new angle of approach to life have been successfully established.

What, after all, is the great outstanding difference between Europe and America? What is the one thing beyond all others that strikes the visitor from the Old World as he travels about the New? Well, I will tell you; it is *youth*. The one great, challenging, striking, outstanding thing in America is the sense of youth everywhere. As a Londoner, the great outstanding difference that I find in America is the spirit of youth. In America everybody is young. Never mind what the calendar may say; here the heart is young. This is the outstanding difference, and it is also the secret of the American Dream, and the American achievement.

Consider the history of the Western Pioneers, for instance, as one of the outstanding examples of this American Spirit. History will some day do justice to that great epic, for such it is, and it will receive the literary treatment that it deserves. It was an essentially individualistic movement planned and carried out by plain men and women of the people, in accordance with the spirit of the American Dream. Without any special training of any kind, and without any real facilities, men and women, lacking everything but the fearless pioneering tradition of America, broke up their homes; packed themselves, and their children, and their parents, and their household goods—their tables and chairs and brooms and pots and pans—into carts, wagons, prairie schooners, or whatever they could get hold of, and set out into an unknown wilderness infested with hostile savages. They fought and endured their way through; worked, and hoped, and prayed, and worked again, until they had firmly laid the foundations of the great new civilization of the West that is yet to be. Very different this, from the military invasions of trained soldiers, led and fed by military experts, that the world had previously been familiar with, or the blind drifting of nomad tribes from one grazing ground to another. It is a human story to rank with the story that Homer sings, and we would recognize it for such if we were not blinded by the familiarity of the framework in which it is set.

The Western Pioneers have done their work and passed off the stage, but other work just as important and just as great is awaiting us their successors. The task which each American has before him is to realize the American Dream in his own life, to the utmost that he is able, by making himself personally free; free in body, and soul, and spirit. Free in body, by demonstrating bodily health. Free in soul, by liberating himself, as far as he can, from every clogging prejudice, whether of party, or race, or creed, or caste; from all the snobbery and limitation that centuries of oppression have burned-in to the life of the Old World. Free in spirit, by rising above all the fetters of personal greed and jealousy, petty spite, mean pride, and small resentments that are the common handicap of humanity in all countries. The American Dream is not a fine theory to be written upon paper, but a life to be lived, for its own sake, and for the sake of the nation, and for the sake of Humanity. The finest Constitution, and the greatest Declaration of Independence ever made are but phrases until they are incorporated into the practical lives of living people. And so, unless you are seeking to embody the American Spirit in your own personal life and conduct, you are no true American, even though you may have authentic Mayflower ancestry.

If you allow yourself to judge the worth of a man by anything except his character, if you discriminate against him for any reason that is outside his own control, you are no true American. If you judge him by his parents, or his connections, or his external conditions, instead of by himself, you are no true American. If you allow yourself to be hampered by any question of precedents or traditions, you are no true American. If you think that any kind of honest work can be degrading, or what is called *infra dig.*, you are no true American. If you would not rather be independent in plain surroundings, than dependent in luxury, you are no true American. If you allow yourself to be dazzled by any exalted Office, or intimidated or hypnotized by pretentious titles or gorgeous uniforms of any kind, you are no true American. And, unless you believe that the poorest boy or girl doing chores around the farm, or playing on the sidewalk of a great city is just as likely—given the opportunity—to turn out to be the greatest soul in the nation as the child who is reared in the lap of luxury, then you are no true American.

The wonderful destiny of the United States is indicated, to those who understand, by an extraordinary system of spiritual symbols which is found running right through the national life. Nowhere else probably is there to be found such a complete and thorough system of symbolism devoted to one particular end. Remember that symbolism is the language of hidden truth. It is the earliest form of language known to man, and it remains the most fundamental. It is the language in which primitive man tried to express vague but tremendous things for which he had no words, and, indeed, no clear ideas. It is the language in which the subconscious speaks to us through the medium of dream and revery; and the transcendent things which the Superconscious has to tell us are transmitted in this language too.

One of the most interesting points about a living symbol as distinct from a mere dead cipher is that it is constantly displayed by all sorts of people who do not in the least suspect what it is that they are doing. They publish and thus help to perpetuate the spiritual symbol under the impression, as a rule, that they are merely using an ornament or decoration that appeals to their artistic sense, or to what they deem to be the fitness of things. Thus it is that symbols of major importance to Humanity are constantly used in the common things and the common actions of everyday life; and until one's attention is drawn to them he passes them by without a second thought. So it is with that collection of most beautiful spiritual symbols which concern the destiny of the United States.

The most important group of these symbols has been so designed as to be in the possession of all American people without any special effort on their part; and in such a way that their publication would not depend upon any particular private interest or special arrangement which might break down, or fail, or disappear.

What is the commonest object circulating throughout the entire nation, in the hands of everybody, rich and poor, in country and town; which is so essential to the conduct of everyday life that nobody fails to make use of it constantly; and which is, at the same time, the accepted token of the very framework of society? Why money, of course. Money, seemingly the most commonplace and matter-of-fact thing in life, is actually the material expression of the most fundamental thing there is, for it is our expression of substance itself, and of the balanced relationship of service between individuals. To understand the true value of money, is to be prosperous and to be free; to misunderstand it means impoverishment in some shape or form, and therefore to be in bondage. To make a god of money is to make a slave of oneself. To ignore money or to misunderstand its true value brings poverty sooner or later. Money, correctly understood, is a device enabling us to make a just return to our fellowman for his service while retaining our own freedom, a thing that any other system of exchange, such as barter, for instance, could never do. The fact that the modern money system is unsatisfactory in practice, and will undoubtedly be radically changed in many important details before very long, does not alter the fact that money in itself is an excellent thing, and the only device which has been invented to guarantee to man his economic freedom.

Now we can understand why it should be that the historical destiny of this country, which we have seen is a spiritual and a liberating one for Humanity, should be spiritually expressed in a system of special symbols; and this explains the wonderful Mystery of the American money. In the ancient Occult Tradition (which is, of course, far older than accepted historical records) a coherent system of symbols that veils for the time being a vital truth from those concerned with it, is known as a Mystery.

The American money is probably the most wonderful and beautiful group of symbols which has ever been put forward among any people to express its national destiny. Various metaphysical students in America have been familiar with some of the symbols for a long time past, but even to those the real Mystery is still veiled. Let us now spend a little time in investigating it. I hold in my hand here, a quarter, or twenty-five cent piece, and I dare say that no object in life is more familiar to most of you;

but have you ever looked at the thing spiritually? Well, the first thing I notice is a beautifully executed female figure, girt with a shield. This figure is beautifully drawn, indicating an upstanding and confident bearing; it is a figure of poise. Corresponding to the shield one would naturally look for a sword in the right hand; but, instead of a material sword, she grasps an olive branch, the symbol of peace and good-will. The woman, of course, is always, in symbology, the soul; and here the soul is armed, not with the sword of Mars, but with the sword of the Spirit, which is the Word of God. If this is not prayer, or spiritual treatment, what is it? Over her head is written the word *Liberty;* and liberty, or freedom from all limitations of sin, sickness, and death, is the final demonstration of the soul that is armed with the Word of Power. Next, my attention is drawn to the slogan which is engraved upon this coin—surely the greatest of all slogans ever composed—*In God We Trust.* Is not this the summing up of all human wisdom? If you could have any legend written upon your own heart; if you, as parents, had the power to write one message into the hearts of your children; would you not wish to write there "In God I Trust." Well, Divine Intelligence has written it for them upon every piece of money which they handle. Note that the greatest danger attaching to the possession of money is the feeling that it may give people of a false security, that it may cause them to rely upon their own power or riches; but Divine Wisdom has here placed the antidote for that poison upon the money itself—*In God We Trust.*

I turn the coin over, and upon the other side I am faced with a motto—and the very greatest of all mottoes too—nothing less than the Cosmic Law itself condensed into three words; nothing less than a whole textbook of metaphysical and spiritual truth in a single phrase; the whole Bible rewritten in a nutshell: *E Pluribus Unum;* One out of Many. Is not this the whole story of man's discovery of the truth about God? At first man thinks himself to be separated from the Divine, and he believes in many gods, but as the Light of Truth gradually dawns in his soul, he passes, first from many gods to the One God, and then on to the final point of knowing his own essential unity with Him, which is salvation. Then he realizes the cosmic truth—"Many but One: One but Many," which is the real meaning behind this motto. This is the whole story of God and man as it is given in the higher teachings; in the Bible for instance, where Jesus says, "I and my Father are One"; and here it is, on every coin that every American man, woman, boy, or girl handles. The whole Bible was written to teach this truth to mankind, and the Metaphysical Truth movement, of which Divine Science is a part, was projected to spread that truth in modern times. There is only one Presence and one Power, but that Presence diversifies Itself in the Universe, and individualizes Itself in man; and yet, without ceasing to be One—*E Pluribus Unum.*

Finally, I take what is perhaps the most beautiful thing of all on this beautiful coin, the wonderful flying eagle, and I ask, what does this eagle flying through the air on those strong and beautiful wings indicate? Well, the eagle is, of course, a symbol of victory; but there is very much more in it than that. An ancient legend concerning the eagle tells us that he has a remarkable peculiarity among birds: When a severe storm occurs, all other birds do one of two things, either they hide from the storm in the lee of any convenient natural shelter, or they try to fight it as long as their strength will hold out. The eagle, however, does neither of these things—*he soars above it.* He neither fights the storm, nor runs away from it, but soars above it. And what, I ask you, is this but Scientific Prayer as we all practice it. In the spiritual teaching we learn, neither to run away from our troubles nor to fight them with will power, but, by turning to God and realizing His ever-presence, to soar above them into the spiritual plane where there is eternal peace and harmony. We know that if only we can do this, even for a few moments, our difficulty, whatever it is, will begin to crumble away, and that by persistence in Scientific Prayer we shall presently overcome it.

But there is something else about this eagle that is exceedingly important. He is not at all as the other eagles that have served as national symbols for other nations in the past. He is not as the Roman eagle, or the Prussian eagle, or the Czarist eagle, or the double-headed eagle of Austria; he is the bald-headed eagle, and wears no material crown. The adoption of the bald-headed eagle as the symbol of the United States is no mere accident, but a spiritual happening of extraordinary occult significance, and it is important to remember that its use is expressly enjoined by an Act of Congress. It signifies nothing less than the power of direct contact with the Divine, or, as we say, the Practice of the Presence of God. Here we need to probe a little below the surface of things, as is always the case when a symbol is particularly important. The top of the head has always been used to signify the faculty of direct contact with God, as distinct from approach to Him through any intermediate channel. This is because that spiritual faculty of the real man is expressed or implied on the physical plane by means of the pineal gland, and on the psychic or etheric plane by the force-center or chakra that lies over the top of the head. Now the whole object of true spiritual development is to realize our essential oneness with God, and as this spiritual faculty develops, we do so more and more. In the Priesthoods of the ancient world the top of the candidate's head was shaven, or made bald, to symbolize this; and here in America we have the bald-headed eagle telling us the same thing in another way—that it is the destiny of the American Nation to lead mankind into the condition where personal freedom and true self-realization will give him at once direct contact with God and true dominion over his own life. That is why this eagle wears no crown of personal or material authority, but teaches the sovereignty of Impersonal Divine Truth.

Many people who start out to seek this true contact with God allow themselves to be diverted either into developing the physical body, in the hope that that will make them spiritual, or into psychic development under the impression that to develop the etheric centers will bring them to God. Nothing could be more mistaken, however. The only true and the only safe development is spiritual development by the Practice of the Presence of God in Scientific Prayer.

I have chosen this particular coin to discuss, because it is the most complete of them all in its presentation of these symbols. The symbols appear again and again, in one form or another, upon all the American money, but in certain cases some of them are omitted. On some quarters, for instance, the head only of the woman appears, and on certain issues of some of the other coins one or other of the mottoes is left out. It is significant that this particular design, the fullest expression of America's destiny, appeared at the moment when America first entered the international field as a World Power, namely, 1916–1917. The quarter was the appropriate piece for this purpose since the dime and the nickel, owing to their small size, offer a somewhat restricted field for display, and the half dollar has, of course, a much smaller general circulation. Is not this quarter in itself a most beautiful and inspiring thing to possess?

The United States has, indeed, produced at various times a large number of beautiful and inspiring coins, usually for the purpose of commemorating some historical event. These form in themselves quite an illustrative history of the nation, and they all embody and proclaim to a greater or less extent the principles we have been considering. Some of them are very remarkable. The St. Gaudens twenty-dollar gold piece, for instance (1908 type onward), is not merely one of the loveliest coins ever struck, but is one of the loveliest objects ever made anywhere. Here the soul is figured as Liberty holding aloft the torch of knowledge, and we know now that true liberty can only come from the understanding of Spiritual Truth, which means the knowledge of the Allness of God. Her foot is placed upon the rock of Truth, and behind her the "sun of righteousness" is arising "with healing in his wings." (Righteousness is right knowledge, or spiritual understanding.) The Capitol at Washington is seen in the distance, signifying, of course, the United States. The whole figure gives an impression of extraordinary poise, and confidence, and carefree exultation. On the other side, the bald-headed eagle naturally appears, also seen against the sunrise. *E Pluribus Unum* and the 13 stars are embossed on the edge of this coin in order to leave more freedom for the designs.

Quite apart from her money, the United States has a wonderful system of national symbolism expressed in other directions. The way in which the number 13, for instance, occurs in her history and in her national emblems is most interesting. We now know that the whole of the material world is really a vast and complicated system of vibrations;

that, and nothing more. The earth you live upon, the house in which you dwell, the body you carry about with you, the food that you eat, and the clothes upon your back, all are but systems and trains of vibration. This means that what we call numbers are really but the indexes of vibrations and have a significance unsuspected by most people. The number 13 is sometimes thought to be what is called "unlucky"; but this is arrant nonsense, for there is no such thing as luck or ill-luck in a universe governed by law. We manufacture our own experience by the kind of thinking that we permit ourselves to indulge in, and that is all about it. Think good, and good will follow; think evil, and evil will follow. That is the rule.

The number 13 is spiritually but an expansion of the number 4, and we find this number emerging in every phase of American History. Thirteen states to start with, and 13 signatures to the Declaration of Independence, 13 stripes on the flag, 13 stars on the money (count them), 13 feathers in the eagle's wing, 13 arrows in his claw, 13 leaves and 13 fruit on the olive branch, 13 rods in the Mace of the House of Representatives, 13 steps in the American pyramid, and 13 letters in the motto *E Pluribus Unum*, are instances that readily occur to mind. The number 4 itself appears as the 4th of July, the day upon which the Declaration of Independence was signed, and upon which the official order was given for a National Great Seal to be prepared. It appears again in the 4th of March, the day upon which a new president was originally inaugurated and we remark that the term of office of a President of the United States is 4 years, a term of office not used in any other country. Now 4, in symbology, stands as the expression of definite, constructive, concrete work; and, as we have seen, it is the historical destiny of the United States to bring the Spiritual Idea into concrete expression on both the mental and the physical planes. This explains why the mottoes on the Great Seal of the United States are: *Novus Ordo Seclorum,* meaning "a new series of ages," or, a new order of things has commenced; and *Annuit Coeptis,* meaning "he (God) has favored our undertakings." Both are from Virgil. Nothing could better describe exactly what America is doing for the world, and the fact that she has a Divine mission.

The Great Seal of the United States contains some of the most extraordinary and interesting symbols in the world. The obverse or front shows the eagle displayed in the ordinary heraldic style, and I have just dealt with the vital significance of the eagle, though it should be noted that he carries an olive branch in his right claw and 13 arrows in his left, denoting that peace and good-will are to be the primary consideration, and defense only the last resort. Metaphysically, the olive branch here stands for the affirmation, and the arrows for the denial, and in Scientific Prayer we must always begin by affirming the Presence of God. The denial, scientifically used, is of great value, but is always secondary in importance to the affirmation.

The unsupported shield that we find here is an heraldic novelty, as most national escutcheons have "supporters" on either side. The American escutcheon rests unsupported on the breast of the eagle, signifying that Scientific Prayer is allsufficient in itself and needs no external or material reinforcement.

The group of 13 stars in the aureole and clouds forms a very unconventional crest or device above the eagle, but this again is a repetition of the announcement that the Spiritual Idea is to come out into concrete definite expression in the United States. The clouds of materiality and misunderstanding are here rolling away from Humanity, and the Sun of Truth is shining out.

Obverse

Reverse

THE GREAT SEAL OF THE UNITED STATES

But the reverse or back of the Seal is, if possible, still more striking and remarkable. (This reverse side seems to be very difficult of access to most people in America. It is not usually shown in the encyclopedias or other works of reference, and for this reason I am having it reproduced herewith.[1] Here we find an unfinished pyramid (notice the 13 steps) the capstone not having yet been lowered into place. Above it and within a triangle appears the ancient symbol of the all-seeing eye. This is, of course, the "Single Eye" of which Jesus spoke. He said: "When the eye is single the whole body is full of light," meaning that when an individual or a nation puts God first, and everything else second, then the whole body, the whole life of that person or that nation, will be healthy and prosperous. The triangle is the symbol of the human soul in which Divine understanding has to appear. The capstone of the pyramid is still unplaced to indicate that man cannot accomplish any real work of himself; but only as the instrument of God—by having the Single Eye. Man has the power of bringing the action of God into play through prayer; but without the Divine action he cannot actually achieve anything. It is because man has so often left God out of his arrangements that all human schemes so far have been transitory. The Single Eye is the "stone that the builders rejected," but it has to become "the head of the corner" in the new building that the American people are erecting.

In the deepest sense, the Single Eye stands for the final spiritual truth of the Allness of God *(E Pluribus Unum)*, which it is the destiny of the United States to make known to the whole world. "And the gospel must first be published among all nations." (Mark 13:10) It is to keep this

---

1. See Note at the end of this chapter.

fact before the American people that the designers of her Great Seal were inspired to place it thereon. It is significant that when it was first designed, this side of the Seal was not received with favor. It was considered inartistic, and even now it is hardly ever shown; and I understand it has not even yet been cut. This is due to the fact that it was not until after the rediscovery of the Spiritual Idea, which, as we have seen, did not happen until the second quarter of the nineteenth century, that its true significance could have been understood by anyone. Now that the knowledge of the Allness of God is at last becoming widespread, the design will gradually come into its own and rank in popularity with the obverse. (The writing of this essay is part of that action.)

This pyramid was designed to be of the same proportions as the Great Pyramid of Egypt, and we are assumed to be looking at the north side, for that is where the entrance to the Great Pyramid is. In a perspective drawing it was necessary to show a second side, and for this purpose the *eastern* side was especially chosen. This is because the East has always stood for illumination or the realization of God. To us mortals the day seems to break in the East, and it is for that reason that many Christian churches as well as the temples of most of the ancient religions were oriented—the altar was placed in the east end of the building so that the worshipers faced the rising sun. The general custom of burying the dead with their feet toward the East that they may face the sunrise is due to the same cause. It is also significant here that the pyramid is the geometrical form that symbolizes Spirit, as it is taken to be the permanent expression of a living flame—the fire principle. Incidentally, the pyramid is a type of stability, for of all solid figures it is the most difficult to overturn. Now we can easily understand that a nation or an individual whose life is sealed with these principles has really made a new beginning, and a very wonderful one, and has nothing to fear.

As a matter of fact, the whole of the American Constitution is, in itself, really a beautiful symbol, almost a diagram, one might say, of the Supreme Truth—*E Pluribus Unum*, Many but One. One but Many, is the supreme and final Cosmic Truth, and this spiritual fact finds a concrete expression in the political arrangement of the United States. They are one, and this unity is the guarantee of the safety and freedom of each; but without ceasing to be one they are many, and this local freedom is the guarantee for the fullest growth and prosperity of each part or State. Without a Federal Constitution, we now see that the United States could not endure. The conditions of life and the consequent needs of the people in such diverse localities as Maine and Arizona, Oregon and Louisiana, are so different; their respective traditions and outlooks are so various; that it is only by complete autonomy in local affairs that they can prosper. The Fathers of the Constitution certainly did not consciously envision the Great Nation and International Power that has grown out of their work; but they were inspired men, whether consciously so or not, and like all inspired men they built better than they knew. This ideal Federal arrangement of corporate unity and individual freedom is, you will see, a perfect expression of the corresponding relationship of God and man. It is instructive to note that the few important mistakes that the American nation has made have in most cases arisen from temporarily forsaking this principle; either by the Federal Government undertaking to do something for the individual States which the Constitution intended them to do for themselves, or by neglecting to do for them something which it should have done. It is curious and interesting to observe that the District of Columbia, centering in the President and, like a sun, surrounded by the forty-eight balanced planetary States, forms a beautiful hieroglyph of the Solar System in which we all live, as well as of the cosmic principle, *E Pluribus Unum.*

Now, does all this mean that I think that the future history of the United States is going to be a simple and easy path of uninterrupted development? No, I do not suppose anything of the kind. The fact is, that a quiet and uneventful life is rather the mark of age and decrepitude than of youth and vigor. It is the destiny of youth to have great problems and great difficulties to tackle and to solve, and it is the glory of youth to have the vision and the energy to do both without fear. When the life of a man or of a nation becomes gentle and uneventful, it means that its work is done; but the work of this nation is only beginning, and I expect, therefore, that in the years ahead of us there will be great problems and difficulties and even dangers to be met and overcome. But I know that as long as the American people are true to themselves, and to the American Dream; as long, that is to say, as they remain united in essentials, so long will they continue to remain undefeated; and so long will they fulfill their destiny of service to the world. Difficulties and problems are good things in themselves because every difficulty overcome is proof of a further advance in consciousness.

Actually there is only one real danger that ever can menace the safety of the United States. Her immense size—she is really a subcontinent—and her ideal geographical location, render her absolutely immune from invasion, other than by raids which might be very costly but could have no permanent effect. There is not, and humanly speaking there cannot be, any enemy on the outside whom she need seriously fear. The only danger that can ever threaten her is that of grave division among her own people. The only real peril that ever can threaten the United States is that one section of the American people should quarrel so bitterly with another section as to make them forget the cause of national unity, and so precipitate an internal conflict. Then indeed, should that happen, the house divided against itself might be made to fall; but in no other way. Should such a thing happen it is not at all impossible that some foreign power would take advantage of her paralyzed condition—for a nation at strife within itself is, of course, militarily paralyzed—to attack her. This all but happened once or twice during the War of North and South; and in days to come owing to the changed conditions of military and naval strategy, such a peril would be a thousand times greater. Again and again in history internal feuds have destroyed nations great and small, but there is every reason to believe that the America people will not be betrayed into this obvious suicidal blunder.

Such a danger cannot arise as long as the American people are careful never to allow party spirit to become so embittered that the destruction of their political enemies seems to be more important than the safety of the country.

However strongly devoted you may be to any particular cause; however strongly opposed you may be to some other cause; the vital thing to remember is that any cause, however good it may be in itself, is secondary in importance to the supreme cause of national unity. Any other doctrine than this is surely plain treason.

An orderly democratic state can only endure as long as the people are prepared loyally to accept the verdict of the majority of their fellow citizens when expressed in a constitutional way, however much it may clash with their feelings; and to support loyally those who are elected to office, whether they like them personally or not.

It is an excellent custom in this country that, after each election, no matter how hotly and bitterly it may have been contested, the defeated candidate sends a telegram of congratulation to his victorious opponent. This custom is a good example of the way in which this truth that we call "Divine Science" has been permeating right through the nation since its birth. This custom is, fundamentally, an affirmation by the defeated party that it is loyal to the Constitution and accepts its spirit even at the most difficult moment.

It is your right, while the election is in progress, to do all that you can to further the success of the party in which you believe. When once the election is over, however, whether it be a minor local event or the National Presidential Election, it is your duty to do all that you can to support and help the man who has been elected, whoever he is. Before the election a candidate is the leader of a party; now he is in office he is the leader of all the people; and this, of course, is the way in which the elected man himself must regard his victory. Any other attitude is really to put a faction before the nation; and if this is not disloyalty, what is it?

These principles will often call for a very great effort of self-control, and will require, in many cases, a great struggle with one's feelings, and with party, family, and other traditions—but how seldom is the higher choice easy for human nature.

From this it naturally follows that any public man, or any newspaper, or any body of people, whatever it may call itself, who may seek unduly to fan the flames of political or sectional bitterness, is to be distrusted. As far as possible, such mischief makers should be ignored, because without material support, their efforts wither away.

Finally, in conclusion, let me say that the more American America can be, the better it will be for America. Let us not copy other countries. Let us not copy Europe, because it is our destiny to be America. Do not copy England; God has done England once, and done it very well, but He does not want to do it again here, because God never repeats Himself. Let us not copy France; God has done France once, and done it very well, and He does not want to repeat that either. Let us not copy Germany, or Italy, or any other country in the world; but be ourselves. If we must make mistakes, in Heaven's name, let us make our own mistakes and not somebody else's. When we do make our own mistakes, we learn a tremendous lot, and, if we suffer too, it is worthwhile, because we learn. But when we make somebody else's mistakes, we suffer just the same, and we learn nothing at all. The more American America can be, the faster she will advance; the better off her people will be; and the more she will help the whole world.

Remember that America is not to be just a new copy of something old, but something quite new, and, therefore, something better than anything that has gone before.

(This chapter is the substance of a lecture delivered in 1932.)

Note: Readers will note that the prophecy made in that lecture that the reverse of the Great Seal (containing the pyramid) would become widely known among the American people has since been fulfilled by the Government issuing a new dollar bill carrying both sides of the Seal.